"As an executive, there is not a day that goes by where I don't apply the coaching skills learned from Christy and her book, whether in the boardroom, as a people leader for my teams, or as a mentor. *The PEER Revolution* is about helping people find their own beautifully unique path, which is so much more impactful than doling out advice or directions."

—ANDREA WESCOTT PASSMAN,
COO Caerus Energy

"*The PEER Revolution* is the perfect blend of Christy's lived experience, deep reflection and extraordinary vision for how coaching can change the world. Her simple yet elegant mindsets, frameworks, tools, and tactics are a must-have in any coach's toolbox. *The PEER Revolution* is certain to be the go-to guidebook for the next generation of coaches, practitioners and human capital teams alike."

—RACHEL BRECHT,
Principal & Director of Organizational Development, TiER1 Performance

"In a world filled with complexity, where the need for curious conversation and human connection is paramount, Christy shares a framework that creates space for us all to learn together. She provides us with models and tools designed to develop a greater sense of individual belonging, and collective common purpose, inside of our organizations and communities. Bringing together a mix of personal storytelling, simple concepts, and reflective questions, this book is exactly what's needed in these complex times."

—DEREK KIRKLAND, PCC, CODC,
Strategic Change, DPR Construction

"*The PEER Revolution: Group Coaching that Ignites the Power of People* is an indispensable strategy manifesto and real-life playbook organizations can draw from for true collaboration and an evolved model of leadership where people thrive. Christy distills decades of insights and offerings to share skillfully-crafted practices, teachings, and tools to guide and call forth the gifts of leaders at all levels."

—ASHLEY GIBBS DAVIS,
Founder, Midtown Associates Coaching & Consulting

"Our employees crave workplaces that foster connection and a sense of belonging. Now more than ever, it's essential that we lead them with empathy and vulnerability. In *The PEER Revolution: Group Coaching that Ignites the Power of People*, Christy provides us with powerful yet practical tools to leverage collective experience and propel our organizations in an inclusive manner."

—ERIC A. BOOTH,
AIA, NCARB, President, Desmone

"Decades of research has shown us the importance of community and peer support to transform our professional and personal lives. We know WHY it matters — but the struggle is HOW to make it happen. *The PEER Revolution* is the step-by-step guide coaches and teams need to harness the strength of the individual and the awesome power of the team."

—CHRISTINE B. WHELAN, PH.D.,
Bestselling Author of Finding Your Purpose, Clinical Professor at the University of Wisconsin, Madison's School of Human Ecology

"The cascading effect of transforming leadership teams is necessary but insufficient. If we are going to transform our organizations through greater courage, confidence, influence, and impact we need to do it at scale. With *The PEER Revolution*, Christy has magically threaded the needle between the power of coaching and transformation that scales."

—GREG MUTCH,
Co-Owner, AG Collaborative

"The power of peer relationships is an invaluable resource. In Christy Uffelman's new book, *The PEER Revolution* she captures the often-untapped power of authentic peer-to-peer connections. Her PEER Coaching Framework provides a timely roadmap for individuals, coaches, managers and leaders to enhance the effectiveness of their most important asset – people."

—AUDREY J. MURRELL, PH.D.,
Professor of Business Administration, Psychology, Public and International Affairs, University of Pittsburgh

"Perceptive, energetic, and provocative. From plausible premises recognizing the 'awesome power of human potential' and the 'intrinsically collaborative nature of the human spirit', Uffelman advocates persuasively for group coaching to develop that potential efficiently. Her book *The PEER Revolution: Group Coaching that Ignites the Power of People* also helpfully suggests techniques for execution."

—CHUCK COHEN,
Chairman Emeritus, Cohen & Grigsby, P.C., Professor, University of Pittsburgh Law School

"Adapting to our new normal, post-pandemic, poses a challenge for today's business leaders. *The PEER Revolution* is a refreshingly forthright, heart-centered guide to support you through this transition period and get you on the right path as you seek novel ways to engage, connect and grow your people and teams. A must read if you are interested in creating inclusive cultures of ongoing learning and improved collaboration."

—LEANNE MEYER,
Author of Climbing the Spiral Staircase: How Women can Navigate Their Careers and Accelerate Success

"The book is very well written, easy to read, and most importantly, full of easy to use frameworks and tools that make sense. The stories and people's personal experiences make the frameworks even more powerful. *The PEER Revolution* provides a multitude of frameworks to help individuals bring their whole self everyday. It starts with creating an environment where individuals can be vulnerable, but with empathy, so that connections can be made. These connections make The PEER Group Coaching Framework even more powerful through greater engagement and self awareness. Sharing these frameworks is a gift we should all embrace."

—JEFF BROWN,
Executive, Independent Family Business Board Director

"Christy shares a crisp framework that is an immediate lift and can be easily applied for coaches and HR practitioners at all stages of their career. However, it is her goal to help the practitioner shape this journey to meet the individual needs of the group in order to elevate the tools from impactful to transformative."

—BETH CODNER,
Chief People Officer

"After 45 years in business, I thought I had seen most of what works in management and leadership, but in her wonderful new book, *The PEER Revolution*, Christy Uffelman presents many new ideas for leaders at all levels to put to immediate practical use in today's organizations."

—JOHN P. SURMA,
Retired Chairman and Chief Executive Officer,
United States Steel Corporation

"As an alumnus of Christy's EDGE Leadership program, I learned that personal advancement happens when you learn to contribute to others' successes and have advanced professionally using the concepts she presents in this book. The secret sauce of a highly recommended corporate leadership development program is written in these pages."

—GODFREY BETHEA, JR. CDP PHR,
Vice President of Equity, People and Culture,
Greater Pittsburgh Community Food Bank

"True Christy—energetic and forward thinking—infused with her personal and professional insights on team development."

—MARY SHIPPY, PhD, PCC.
CEO, Align Leadership

"The PEER Revolution is a must read for all internal coaches who are looking for new and innovative ways to develop high potential leaders in their organization."

— BARB HICKEY, SR.
Talent Development Manager, Black Box Corporation

"Our #1 job as leaders is to be there for our teams. Christy provides a powerful roadmap to create an environment of vulnerability, empathy, and belonging that allows your team to thrive. *The PEER Revolution* inspires with a lot of real-world examples, equipping you to be a better leader and coach!"

—LINDSEY FARRELL,
Global VP- Supply Chain, Ops, and Quality- Komatsu Mining Corp.

"Christy does an amazing job outlining highly effective methods to empower people and to build trust in today's world. Christy's methods are practical and straightforward, and they work. If you are as concerned as I am about attracting and retaining talent, I recommend reading *The PEER Revolution: Group Coaching that Ignites the Power of People.* The book will provide a perspective that you and your team will greatly appreciate."

—TROY GEANOPULOS,
CEO, The Efficiency Network (TEN)

"In a rapidly changing world Christy rebrands and re-energizes peer coaching by empowering people to support and challenge themselves and others in pursuit of growth and understanding through the PEER Group Coaching. This non-prescriptive model will not provide answers but will gently and intentionally guide one through challenging the status quo, changing perspectives, and establishing a deeper understanding of self awareness."

—SHELBY BAKER,
Executive

"Christy is passionate about developing leaders and 'lighting their candles' so they can do the same for others. She is a consummate learner, teacher, motivator, connector, and relationship builder. Onward!"

—KIM TILLOTSON FLEMING, CFA ®,
Chairman and CEO, Hefren-Tillotson, Inc.

"Having experienced Christy Uffelman's pure magic first hand, she has unsurprisingly captured the genie into a bottle that will benefit any leader who is brave enough to break into the full potential of individuals, small teams, or entire organizations. The power that lies within these pages forces talent inward to recognize their own fire, leading to incredible truth and outcomes!"

—DARAH KIRSTEIN,
Technologist, Entrepreneur & Mom of 4

"Nothing of enduring significance was created in isolation by one person. Everything of value was built on something that preceded it, and by a community of people that nurtured it. Christy Uffelman personifies that reality in her own life, and amplifies its importance in her book, *The PEER Revolution*, to all who desire their workplaces to be fertile soil for flourishing."

—SALEEM GHUBRIL,
Executive Director, The Pittsburgh Promise

"Christy has loads of experience leading organizational change using this powerful PEER Group Coaching Framework. She helps everyone, regardless of role, curate belonging and create deeper team connections."

—CARI WILLIAMS,
Global Social Responsibility Leader, DPR Construction

"As a leader, I am continually searching for new ways to develop my team, but I sometimes feel like I'm doing the same things without seeing different results. With *The PEER Revolution* I see an opportunity to use the strength of a group to empower individuals to grow personally and professionally."

—RICK SAULLE,
National Sales Manager

THE
PEER
REVOLUTION

GROUP
COACHING THAT
IGNITES
THE POWER OF
PEOPLE

CHRISTY UFFELMAN, MHCS, BCC

PRESS

The PEER Revolution:
Group Coaching that Ignites the Power of People

Copyright © 2022 Christy Uffelman

Published by StoryBuilders Press

ISBN: 978-1-954521-01-8. First edition.

TABLE OF CONTENTS

Foreword: S = GB + GP + f 1

Introduction 5

SECTION ONE: THE REVOLUTION **9**

Chapter 1: The Power of Peer Relationships 11

Chapter 2: A Coaching Revolution 33

Chapter 3: Challenging the Script 51

Chapter 4: The Growth Mountain 75

Chapter 5: PEER Coaching in Action 97

SECTION TWO: THE FRAMEWORK **121**

Chapter 6: The Container 123

Chapter 7: Self-Awareness 161

Chapter 8: Outcomes 183

Chapter 9: Relevant Content 201

Chapter 10: The Practice Arena 225

Chapter 11: 1:1 Coaching 247

SECTION THREE: THE SALE **283**

Chapter 12: Selling PEER Coaching 285

Chapter 13: Mistakes to Avoid 311

Conclusion 329

About the Author 332

Acknowledgments 333

FOREWORD

S = GB + GP + f

Success = *Growing* the *Business* + *Growing* the *People* + *Having fun* along the way.

This was an equation I made into a logo for my first executive role serving as Director of Corporate Investments for a 45-person department back in the early 1990s. My experiences since then have confirmed that "Growing the People" is a quintessential factor for driving the success of any enterprise. But how do we grow people in a scalable way?

I met Christy Uffelman on Thursday, November 17, 2016, at the Women on Boards 2020 forum held at the Wyndham Grand in downtown Pittsburgh. My first impression? *Wow! What an incredible bundle of positive energy—like lightning in a bottle.*

Since that first meeting, I have had the opportunity to watch Christy command gatherings of more than 300 aspiring executives who envision themselves serving on a corporate board one day. I have also had the privilege of collaborating with Christy on some of her group coaching engagements and witnessing firsthand the PEER approach captured in this book. It was big-time fun, watching seasoned and junior executives alike lean in, become vulnerable, and allow themselves to access more of their potential for leadership development and upward mobility in their companies. I came away from those PEER Group Coaching sessions having gained way more than I gave and hope to be invited to participate in more sessions soon.

All of these interactions with Christy have helped me in the coaching work I do with diverse groups of people. One group comprises the most senior members of one of the branches of the U.S. Armed Forces, for whom I conduct a leadership series entitled "World Class Performance: The Role of Leadership, Process, and Talent." Another group comprises company founders seeking to scale their companies to becoming the industry standard bearers in their respective markets. A third group comprises public company board directors seeking to become the best board directors they can possibly be. In all those settings, I have the privilege of working with high-performing people seeking ways to be even better. The power of peer relationships is reflected in each of these settings as leaders learn from one another's experiences and support one another through the sharing of opportunities, knowledge, and network.

I love that the insights and tenets of *The PEER Revolution* offer a transformational way of thinking about and executing on the construct of coaching. The book codifies the approach Christy has incorporated into the incredibly successful coaching practice she has built with EDGE Leadership. Yet again, I am impressed that Christy has chosen not to build a wall around PEER Group Coaching and treat it as proprietary, but rather to make it "open source" so more people can benefit from the approach.

Getting people to change and grow is difficult. However, *The PEER Revolution* provides a map along with road signs and guardrails to allow more people and companies to unleash the fullness of their talent.

The key observations that I would share are that the PEER Group Coaching works and works better than traditional approaches to coaching, and that it is amazingly scalable. This is a critical enabling feature for organizations that want to broadly affect their most important asset, their people.

Christy's PEER Group Coaching Framework resonates with me and aligns with my own experiences. Creating the **Container**, for example, is foundational and establishes a spirit of trust and cooperation early on in the process. Likewise, **Self-Awareness** makes growth possible. The self-selection that takes place for each of the Forums that African American Director's Forum (AADF) hosts demonstrates that each person must begin by acknowledging their need for growth or desire to help others grow.

Setting personal **Outcomes**, such as obtaining a seat on a for-profit or non-profit Board, always defines the growth experiences and informs the selection of **Relevant Content**. Vertical knowledge transfer is an essential part of the process, and I both bring in guest speakers and have served as a Guest Mentor to activate this part of the process.

The **Practice Arena** is where people begin to apply what they learn, bringing people together to learn best practices and benefit from one another's experiences. Finally, the value of 1:1 Coaching cannot be underestimated. I love that Christy focuses on teaching cohort members to develop their own 1:1 Coaching skills. In fact, I have had the privilege of doing some 1:1 Coaching with Christy herself. These "coach the coach" sessions have been hugely valuable to me personally and professionally.

For those professional coaches looking for a way to improve their effectiveness, create more satisfied clients, and grow their practices, *The PEER Revolution* is a must-read. It combines a practitioner's framework with Christy's personal learning journey in a way that brings the concepts to life and makes the book immensely readable and usable.

Whether you are formally in the role of coaching or are in a position that influences an organization's approach to coaching, strap in—you are in for an enjoyable and provocative read!

—**DAVID MOTLEY**
Pittsburgh, PA

David Motley serves on multiple public company boards, has founded companies across several industries, is a Managing Partner of Black Tech Nation Ventures, and lectures at the Navy War College.

INTRODUCTION

I t is my lifelong mission to ensure that people feel less alone by making connections that matter.

Keeping this in mind, when I reference gender and use pronouns in this book, I do so with an inclusive intention. If I say *women*, or use variations of the pronoun *she*, for example, I am referring to anyone who identifies as female. Likewise, when I say men or use variations of the pronoun he, I am referring to anyone who identifies as male. Wherever possible, I use the most inclusive pronouns available to us at the writing of this book *they/them*.

With that inclusivity in mind, I often make references that are relevant to the external coach, that is the person who works as a vendor from outside an organization, coming alongside to help the people in the organization grow. However, the internal coach, the person within the organization who also helps people in the organization grow, can tweak the application to make use of those same insights. In some places, I may state how to do so explicitly. In others, I may make suggestions. So when I talk about "clients," know that I am referring to whoever it is that you serve. Regardless of your position, whether you are an external or internal coach or a people leader who wants to apply these concepts to curate belonging and connection on your team, I trust your ability to apply what you learn to your specific scenarios in fresh and creative ways.

That being said, any leader can learn from and apply what I share in this book to increase their influence and impact. In fact, every single person reading this book has the power to be a coach. That reality is at the heart of the PEER Revolution.

I also want to be clear that many of the tools and techniques I use within the PEER Group Coaching Framework did not originate with me. They were inspired by a range of diverse experiences with diverse people. Many techniques began with a seed planted by one person, grew as it was watered by input from another, and flourished within experiences with still others. I have tried to give credit where I could discern a distinct source, but also want to be authentic and acknowledge my reliance on a host of creative leaders on whose shoulders I am able to stand.

I picked up many of these nuggets and best practices along my own journey of personal and professional development— both as a student of group coaching and as a teacher of it—and now want to share what has worked for me in my flourishing coaching practice to help you expand your impact as well.

I simply could not offer much value to you here were it not for my business partner and husband Kevin. So whenever I speak of *we* and *our*, know it truly has been a collaborative effort to bring this PEER Revolution to life through our company, EDGE Leadership. In addition to him keeping us financially afloat while I initially started the new enterprise, we were so successful within two years that he came on board to manage the operations of the company. Because I had been a solopreneur before, I knew what was not in my natural strength zone. Kevin stepped in with expertise as a seasoned manager, team builder, and business leader. We absolutely would not be where we are today if it weren't for him. His excellent management has allowed me to live in my creative research and development space, tinkering, building, playing, and (much to his frustration sometimes) endlessly iterating!

More than anything, I want you to ask yourself, what if there was a way to bring the human experience to new heights, break through the boundaries to success, and create collective personal and professional transformation?

No matter where or how you may do it, I want you to empower yourself to curate connection and belonging and maximize human potential wherever you find opportunity so you can truly make a lasting impact. Using the PEER Technology® Group Coaching Framework in the following pages, you'll discover how to harness the incredible power of connection and ignite the flames of collective success.

My candle has been lit by countless others. Now I bring this PEER Framework and collection of best practices to help you not only light your candle but also ignite the candles of others, because a flame loses nothing in lighting another.

Together we can change the world. This is just the beginning....

Onward.

—CHRISTY UFFELMAN, MHCS, BCC

SECTION ONE:
THE REVOLUTION

1

THE POWER OF PEER RELATIONSHIPS

"You cannot teach a man anything. You can only help him discover it within himself."

— GALILEO

About fifteen years ago, on a rainy Tuesday morning, I pulled into the parking lot at work and I.Gave.Up. If I'm being really honest, the giving up process actually started about five hours earlier, when my four-year old son woke up in the middle of the night. He couldn't sleep. As a single mother, that meant neither could I. But I had an important presentation to give that day. So I got him off to daycare that morning (without checking his temperature) because, well, I did what I felt I had to do to make it all work.

I pulled into the parking lot of the industrial company I was working for at the time and paused to take a deep breath. As

I did, the sky opened up, and sheets of rain—we're talking *torrential downpour*—started falling. It was right about then that I realized I had taken my umbrella into the office a few days ago, and it was still there *in* my office, *inside* the building.

Did I mention I had spent an hour on my hair and makeup that morning for the presentation I was about to give to the CEO (my boss) and the executive team—with a fussy toddler on the floor next to me? I sat in my car watching guy after guy hop out of pickup trucks and run into the glass-enclosed lobby, barely pausing to shake off the water. Finally, when the rain showed no sign of stopping, I took off my suit jacket and grabbed my briefcase, determined to use it as a makeshift umbrella. I clutched it over my head as I jumped from the car and dashed for the safety of the dry lobby.

As I skidded into the lobby, the kind receptionist's eye met mine. Without a word, I could feel her pity. She knew my situation better than anyone. I was the first female manager the company ever had. While I was grateful to work for a family of truly great men who saw the value I brought to their business, I had a long road ahead when it came to earning credibility with my peers—all men with stay-at-home wives running their households.

I am sure the receptionist knew the questions that were, no doubt, being asked about me, a twenty-something single mom who joined the company with zero experience in that industry and who spent most of her days having private coaching conversations behind closed doors with male managers. I put an encouraging smile on my face, trying to assure her (and myself) that I was totally fine, shook off as much water as I could, and headed to my office, where I shut the door behind me and promptly burst into tears.

I almost quit eight times in the first two years. Things that I never expected to be difficult were incredibly so. And the week prior, I had just received the promotion to become the first female on the executive team. My presentation that day would be my first to a room full of new peers.

I was trying to push forward without acknowledging the struggles I faced. I thought I could somehow, some way, find a way to do it all. I could meet every expectation and overcome any barriers. I could grit my teeth, try harder, and figure it out. But in that office at that moment, I ran into reality and felt like I had done a faceplant.

I had refused to acknowledge all the challenges I faced and had unconsciously let those challenges define me. Only by retaking control of my story could I rewrite the ending. So yes, I gave up that day.

I gave up thinking I had to do it all myself.

IT ALL STARTS WITH CONNECTION

One thing I knew for sure—I needed to find someone who had been there, done that. I needed to connect with some women leaders who knew how to navigate this challenge. I started looking around the region. The first thing I learned seems rather obvious now: you can't ask a stranger to be your mentor. The answer is almost always going to be *no*, or at least it was in my case.

So I did the next best thing—I started going anywhere professional women met, hopping from group to group all over the city. Although those meetings were mostly enjoyable, they often felt inauthentic and networky. What I was really craving was genuine connection within a peer group.

Seeking genuine connection was so purposeful for me because I believe in the awesome power of human potential. Everyone boldly starts in their careers as if we're on a path of personal achievement. We try; we fail; we overcome. We learn, work hard, and receive accolades for a job well done *as individuals*. We each tend to view the world as if we're in the spotlight alone—especially early in our careers—with all the attention and responsibility resting on one set of shoulders. And yet as we grow, somehow achieving great results simply isn't enough any more. It doesn't fan our flames the way it once did. We begin to feel stuck.

It is in this crucial pivot point where the focus must shift from seeking personal achievements to searching for ways to contribute to others. It's the difference between one match burning alone in the darkness and many flames burning together to light the world.

I began to learn this truth quite inadvertently. As I went from one women's event to the next, I started finding amazing women from whom I wanted to learn. In fact, the man who would later become my husband, Kevin, told me during that time it was as if I were collecting women like jewels on a crown. I had found relationship and connection, but I had not yet discovered the space of learning I needed.

What I wanted was development alongside other women, a space to learn what was working for them, what wasn't working so well, and why. And to apply those best practices in my life. I needed an intentional learning framework with those critical relationships built into it. When I couldn't find the peer learning I wanted, I realized I would need to create it.

I was also looking for accountability. After all, if I was going to be big and bold, and the first female VP this company had ever seen, what responsibility did I have to every other woman in that company? Even at twenty-nine years of age, these women would look to me. But the truth was, I had no clue how to inspire and bring value to them. Plus, the story I had been telling myself was that I couldn't because I just wasn't good enough.

The very first peer group I created in 2007 was a cohort of working mothers just like me, because honestly, that was where I felt I needed the most support at the time. We had mothers across the generations, with children in kindergarten (like mine), middle school, high school, and even college. We had married moms and single moms, new moms and seasoned ones. We got together on a monthly basis and followed a simple peer-learning, Mastermind format (yes, I'll explain how we did that in the pages to come).

We quickly became a part of a circle of contribution, celebrating each other's successes, supporting one another in our challenges, and giving each member space to practice asking for help. No doubt you've heard the expression, "Two heads are better than one." This universal truth describes in the simplest terms how collective thinking can produce greater results than any one individual's thought or idea. When each of our individual and unique perspectives work in harmony with others, we get collective engagement, empowerment, and change. We learn that everyone, especially those we may not have expected, has something to contribute, because each voice carries with it a lifetime of experience, education, wisdom, and insights.

This early group experience was the spark that soon began to burn brightly. Although I didn't set out to do it when I began that first peer group, the journey ultimately led me to create an innovative approach to group coaching in 2013 called PEER Technology®. It stands for Partnership, Experience, Exposure, and Reflection.

P

Partnership: The idea that it's not all about me. Instead, it's about me in partnership with another. We show up together, as partners, contributing to and holding one other accountable.

E

Experience: It unfolds based on an individual's personal Outcomes, as well as the Outcomes of the peer group as a whole.

E

Exposure: This is about practicing vulnerability and embracing new ideas through mentoring and coaching. It's about exposure to innovation, contributing to and receiving an infinite flow of knowledge.

R

Reflection: It is vital for people to look at how we are currently showing up, how we are getting in our own way, and what we are going to choose to do differently. It's a space of learning and growth.

At the heart of this revolutionary PEER Framework of group coaching are intentional, developmental cohorts that leverage peer-centered coaching in an environment of equity, and inclusion. These intentional peer groups (developmental cohorts) focus on cooperative personal and professional development. They leverage the intrinsically collaborative nature of the human spirit.

"These intentional peer groups (developmental cohorts) focus on cooperative personal and professional development. They leverage the intrinsically collaborative nature of the human spirit."

Although I didn't fully realize it at the time I was developing the Framework (selfishly, to serve my own needs), as I look back now, more than fifteen years later, I see I was tapping into something powerful. The global community seeks diversity and inclusion. Above all else, each person wants to offer something unique as part of the whole. This Framework has proven to be truly transformative, but it didn't happen immediately.

THE FLAMES OF COOPERATIVE THINKING

What was unique about the initial working mothers group was that we had mothers from all across the spectrum. It was amazingly powerful (and yet invisible to me at the time) that this first peer group experience included women from different places and spaces in life. As a result of the rich diversity of experiences, we all benefited from both vertical and horizontal knowledge transfer taking place at exactly the same time.

When I, as the mother of a kindergartner, bemoaned what was happening in my life and made myself feel guilty about struggling, a more seasoned mother stepped up to say, "I hear you. I've been there. But what you're worrying about isn't actually super important. And I think what you said earlier about what happened on the playground last week may be more critical to focus on. Here's why." That level of honest, experienced insight might not have happened if we hadn't had a safe space to be vulnerable with a diverse group of women.

The success of that first group spawned a high-potential women's group in the Pittsburgh, Pennsylvania region. Young women across companies and industries gathered in my kitchen on a monthly basis to share best practices. Because we were truly a peer group based on career-experience level (all in our late 20s to mid 30s), we quickly found out that peer learning has an inherent limitation. We don't know what we don't know! We had to give ourselves permission to become vulnerable and ask for help outside the cohort.

As I reflected on what made the working mother's group so successful, I saw the concept of "vertical knowledge transfer" clearly for the first time. I knew we needed to add an additional layer. By leveraging the power of our collective networks, the participants themselves amplified our ranks with executives from across the region who came to share their best practices with us. We chose topics we were stuck on, and these Guest Mentors, as I came to call them, met our vulnerability with vulnerability by engaging in an authentic dialogue with us. Our little cohort blossomed and started to get visibility with executive leaders working in both corporate and not-for-profit organizations across industries. Soon, we had a waiting list of executives who wanted to engage with our cohort. (I'll definitely share more about how these Guest Mentors work!)

About eighteen months later, a national mentoring organization called Strong Women, Strong Girls (SWSG) asked if I would be interested in building a leadership development experience pro bono for them based on what I had learned in these group coaching sessions. An executive on their board of directors had served as a Guest Mentor. They wanted to get more young, Millennial women volunteering with the organization in a way that would create sustainable corporate giving for their nonprofit.

So, with two cohorts under my belt, I built my first "official" group coaching experience in Pittsburgh, layering in peer learning, Guest Mentors, and coaching. At the time, in 2009, the SWSG framework included professional women mentoring college women, and college women mentoring at-risk girls in grades three through five. I decided to challenge the status quo a bit. Rather than expecting these women to have it all together and tell others what to do (that's often how we define mentoring, but as I mentioned earlier, I was struggling to do that myself as a twenty-something), I wanted to teach them *how to coach*. We built a leadership development experience where companies would sponsor a high-potential woman to become a part of this unique group coaching experience (creating annual revenue flow for SWSG). Not only would the young leader herself gain valuable coaching skills, but her team and the company would also benefit.

We had so much success in Pittsburgh that SWSG asked me to expand my volunteer work, sit on their national board of directors, and help them to launch another high-potential women's cohort in Boston—and another in Miami! I could see this peer-centered group-coaching dynamic was both unique and powerful. I knew I had to figure out how to bring it into more people's lives. While my day job as the head of HR and L&D certainly challenged my brain, I realized this group coaching work was filling my soul in a way I never could have imagined.

I have always been someone who was driven to explore new possibilities and eagerly tackled challenges. Prior to accepting the position in the industrial company, I had explored the entrepreneurial world in my mid-twenties as well, gaining valuable real-world experience. My experiences accelerated my learning curve (and bumps and bruises). I knew organizations around the world needed this group coaching approach to take success to the next level. Plus, this new PEER Framework created a space for organizational knowledge transfer, meeting a critical need in the marketplace in advance of the impending Boomer retirement. I realized that, in thinking of how I could become a better leader personally, I had unwittingly sparked a coaching revolution to ignite a power in people unlike anything else out there.

COLORING IN COAL MINES

After launching EDGE Leadership in 2013, I knew the PEER Framework was successful for groups of women, but I needed to know how it could work for other demographics of people. That's when I met internal coach Michelle. Michelle Buczkowski grew up in a small town outside of Pittsburgh. As a first-generation college educated person with a blue-collar upbringing, she thought she was going to be a wedding planner, but ended up getting into the staffing industry in a recruiting position. From there, she moved on to succession planning and building a Talent Management department.

Sometimes the bigger (and faster) your career growth is, the more it feels like life is hitting you. The big transformation happened for Michelle when, thanks to her PEER experience, she realized the world was not coming at her, she was coming at the world. This realization changed her entire perspective and opened her eyes to the fact that she was in control of what her life and work could look like.

At the age of twenty-six, Michelle sat in a lonely office on the third floor in a male-dominated industry. The CEO and executives sat on the fourth floor. With both metaphorical and literal distance between them, she felt invisible. She did not project any validity or credibility behind her voice, but that was about to change.

The energy company she was working for at the time was in a growth mode, but they had a very traditional mentality. Advancements in technology led the company (and the industry as a whole) to hire very few people for nearly twenty years, then everyone started retiring all at the same time. Looking at the age demographics, they had a lot of highly experienced people from an older generation, along with a lot of fresh new recruits to replace them, but few people in the middle.

With so many senior staff retiring, they had to pipeline talent into senior level positions very quickly. But the energy industry is highly-regulated. To effectively fill empty seats, new hires needed certain training and certifications. The hard part was figuring out how to find shift supervisors and well-paid managers from a pool of twenty-somethings with engineering degrees coming straight out of school. How would they replace the fifty-five-year-old with all the institutional knowledge who is taking a well-deserved retirement package and benefits early and heading off to the beach?

When I first met Michelle in 2013, she invited me into the windowless basement of the company's headquarters. We sat across the table from one another as she told the story of how the company got as far as it did. We worked together to get a plan in motion. The plan was to create a cohort-based leadership program and have a meeting every month, with a goal to turn supervisors and directors into vice presidents. The only problem was, she didn't have a strong enough pool of talent a layer below that to turn into supervisors or directors. In order to have a pipeline, it's vital to actually have the pipe.

We co-created what a PEER Group Coaching experience would look like for them, and launched it with a cohort made up of twenty- to thirty-year-old Millennial men. We met the cohort where they were, in their environment, 800 feet below the Earth's surface, literally in a coal mine. It became our underground cohort classroom. There would be a few challenges along the way. For example, Michelle had to convince the superintendent of the mine to let her take yarn and construction paper underground to use for creative expressions in one of the cohort activities. (It could not have been easy to explain they were going to be coloring in his coal mine that day.)

The reality is, cohort members in the PEER experience have to come to it on their own. As a coach, you can't force people to become vulnerable and fully invested in the experience.

Michelle watched the men tentatively start joining in. She watched them getting closer and closer to opening up and being more vulnerable. Soon, the entire experience became an exciting journey, watching when the different parts of the model clicked with each cohort member.

What was the result of the experience? When Michelle surveyed them after the full experience ended, the data showed exactly how much the men in the cohort had changed as a result of the experience. Self-admittedly, they became better husbands, fathers, partners, sons, and brothers. As the men gave themselves permission to become vulnerable, offered and received support, and discovered their Outcomes, they transformed.

Men sat right in front of Michelle with tears running down their faces. One told her the story of how he adopted a child and the struggles they had gone through with infertility. Another spoke about his family life growing up, and why being so hard on his crew at work was just ingrained into who he was and what had been modeled for him. He realized that abandoning that negative energy almost felt like abandoning part of his heritage.

Really quickly, Michelle saw that by growing as a complete person, the men in the cohort started to show up differently as leaders. And as so often happens for coaches using the PEER Framework, she realized how much she was growing through the process as well. They leaned on one another and admitted they didn't have all the answers. They asked for help. They were on the radar for promotions sooner than expected. And she went from feeling alone in her third-floor office to feeling like she had the entire city of Pittsburgh rooting for her in a few short years.

EXPANDING HUMAN POTENTIAL

When it comes to maximizing potential, there's a paradox. On one hand, it's natural for people to feel the need to prove credibility and competence in the workplace, to look as though they know what they're doing and deserve to be there. If you have coached for any length of time, you've encountered many people who mistakenly think vulnerability demonstrates weakness or exposes inadequacy. But in reality, there exists a true need for a safe space, a place for people to practice the kind of vulnerability that fosters genuine growth and improvement.

I have a question for you: whether you coach corporate leaders 1:1 in-house (as an internal coach within an organization or as a people leader with your team) or provide those coaching services and training to businesses as an external vendor, can your coaching framework routinely help people foster real growth in a way that is *not* dependent on you?

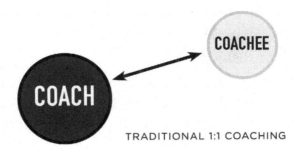

TRADITIONAL 1:1 COACHING

Don't get me wrong. There is a valid and important place for 1:1 Coaching, even within the PEER Framework. But if all of your coaching depends on you being present, you can only be in so many places at once. There are only so many coaching time slots on your calendar. And you can only share what is in *your* knowledge bank.

But what if you could add to your coaching services the ability to coach many people all at once—by empowering them to coach one another and themselves? Interested? I hope so, because that is only the beginning of the benefits of this revolution in PEER Group Coaching.

I invite you to ask yourself: are a lot of your coaching clients in similar developmental spaces, but within a diverse peer group? How could you structure a tested-and-true coaching experience for them?

Could you use an effective way to leverage a wide range of skill sets to achieve a common goal in an organization or industry, all while maximizing the company's coaching and training budget to create win-win scenarios?

How can you integrate experience and create intentional space for vertical knowledge transfer without trying to turn seasoned executives and internal subject matter experts into "trainers" wielding PowerPoints and worksheets?

If any of these scenarios interest you, stay tuned. And that's not even counting the passive revenue cycle for external coaches using this PEER Group Coaching Framework. (If you like making money while making an impact, you're going to *love* that!)

Plus, if you're like most coaches I know, you would prefer not to focus on selling. You may even see sales as a necessary evil. So when I tell you this PEER Framework is easier to sell to companies (and for more than you are likely getting for your services now) do your ears perk up? Good. Because I'll not only show you how to do it, step-by-step, but also reveal secrets to doing it well, and a few mistakes I've made (so you don't have to).

If you are an internal coach within an organization, these experiences will help you magnify your impact to your CHRO and have greater influence in building a sustainable pipeline of talent to the top. For you, it will have the additional benefit of saving the organization money by not needing to bring in external coaches and, like Michelle did, creating an organic space for mentoring and sponsorship to take root—all while vertical and horizontal knowledge transfer fuels your talent pipeline. A healthy pipeline has never been more important for HR professionals and coaches pivoting in response to crises like a global pandemic, confronting related workforce challenges, and learning to leverage virtual technologies to sustain culture.

Perhaps you are a corporate leader trying to devise the growth path for people in your organization. You may be a leader in HR or Talent Management who has done a good bit of coaching yourself, and now the company is looking to you to help coach other team members to success. You already know how hard it is to increase employee retention and drive engagement. You have to be concerned about employee mobility, how to promote people with confidence, and how to fully develop and engage coworkers. You may have executives who want to contribute but don't know how. They're stuck in old-school "mentoring programs" that feel like Match.com-gone-wrong and leave them feeling drained and inauthentic. The good news: you can use the PEER Framework to elevate and expand human potential no matter how busy your leaders are.

Another critical piece of good news: this PEER Framework is perfectly suited for virtual environments to bring people together across diverse life experiences, viewpoints, and geography. More than ever, as many leaders lead remote teams, we have to be able to connect people in ways never possible before.

But now you can do just that.

IGNITE: BEST PRACTICES

✓ Acknowledging challenges in life is important. When people refuse to do this, we unconsciously let those challenges define us.

✓ A shift must take place from seeking individual achievements to searching for ways to contribute to others. It's the difference between one match burning alone in the darkness and many flames burning together to light the world.

✓ When each of our individual and unique perspectives work in harmony with others, we get collective engagement, empowerment, and change.

✓ A safe space is necessary for vulnerability. Ideally, a place for people to practice opening up, a place that fosters real growth and development.

✓ You can add to your coaching services the ability to coach many people all at once—by empowering them to coach one another and themselves.

✓ You can use the PEER Framework to elevate and expand human potential no matter how busy your leaders are.

✓ The PEER Framework is perfectly suited for virtual environments. As many leaders lead remote teams, it's important to connect people using innovative and alternative means.

THOUGHT SPARKS

1. *Can you think of a time when collective thinking increased productivity or success in your business or organization? What made it so powerful?*

2. *How have you intentionally developed a safe space within your current coaching program that promotes vulnerability? What's worked well for you? What hasn't so much?*

3. *How effectively do you currently employ group coaching? Where do you see that it could improve? What's the benefit you could gain from layering it in with what you already do? With whom? Why?*

4. *In what ways might your coaching benefit from being able to impact many people all at once—by empowering them to coach one another and themselves?*

2

A COACHING REVOLUTION

"Individually, we are one drop.
Together, we are an ocean."

—RYUNOSUKE SATORO

As a Millennial, I'm really big on connection and collaboration. Growing up, I didn't sit in neatly-arranged rows in a classroom. Instead, my generation was part of a new initiative that arranged classrooms into pods where children learned and shared ideas cooperatively. I learned the same way in college, and it's how I continue to learn today. It's not just a neat idea or a fad in learning styles—it actually works!

When I started my first career out of college in surgical equipment sales, I worked for Johnson & Johnson. I was in operating rooms with surgeons all day, every day, selling new instruments to repair people's bodies. Because I was very good at what I did, I was flagged after a few years as a high-potential and given a stretch assignment to help develop new talent within my region. I soon discovered my favorite part of my job was mentoring new hires.

Without having the words for it, I fell in love with adult development. As a naive twenty-four year old, I thought I wanted to be a manager, because a manager was all about developing people (or so I thought). However, at Johnson & Johnson, in order to move up, you had to move out.

I soon shifted to another global healthcare company, Bayer, because I didn't want to move out (away from Pittsburgh). This time I led a team selling multi-million dollar equipment to hospitals. I was able to convince Bayer that I was the perfect fit for a sales management position, even though I had no official management experience under my belt. Unfortunately, in less than a year, I went down in flames. As I have since learned, what makes someone a successful sales rep does not necessarily make them a successful sales manager.

Luckily, Bayer didn't fire me, although they certainly could have. I couldn't hold anyone accountable for results. I wanted everyone to like me. I often found myself doing the actual tasks of my team to ensure that things got done "right." However, that experience opened my eyes to the area of Learning and Development. I discovered there was an entire field focused on developing others, and it had a name—coaching.

Moreover, I discovered I could have succeeded if only I had a way to learn from others, a vehicle for knowledge transfer. Was this failure all mine? No. As those of you who are internal coaches know all too well, our companies have a responsibility to grow talent for the next level of their leadership.

I realized that as an ambitious—and perhaps slightly over-confident—Millennial, I needed to step out of the spotlight, stop thinking only about my individual achievement, and start looking at light in a very different way. I needed to start seeing light as the product of a flame, because a flame burns brighter when united with others. At that time, I needed space to be inspired by the insights and best practices of a diverse experience pool with whom I could collaborate and learn.

Ultimately, I left Bayer to open my first coaching company, Red Zebra Consulting, in 2003. After a few years, I was recruited by a family-owned business in the industrial space to come in-house as an internal coach to help them create their next cultural iteration. They were in the midst of a generational transition from father to several sons.

I went from the Director of Organization Development to the VP of Human Resources within the first two years. It was shortly after the promotion that my mad dash through the rain had occurred on that Tuesday morning. My role was not only to support the second generation of leadership as they took the company to the next level, but also to be an in-house coach for their executives and high-potentials.

I was also responsible for designing sustainable, formal mentoring and soft skills training programs within the company. As the head of HR, I was the one in charge of hiring external coaches and evaluating leadership programs, but the programs that vendors offered at that time, in the early 2010s, seemed ineffective and outdated. So I began to experiment with different approaches.

I spent seven years working there, learning more than I ever dreamed. Throughout my time, I learned the value of transparency and maintaining a robust, honest dialogue in business. I can honestly say I wouldn't be doing what I am doing today if it weren't for the generosity and advocacy I experienced from that leadership team.

After leaving the company, I created the PEER Group Coaching Framework built on my struggles, my needs, and my stories, after having unexpectedly beta-tested it by doing pro bono work with non-profits like Strong Women Strong Girls (SWSG). I then began using it within Fortune 500 companies to transform workplace culture, make EBRGs (Employee Business Resource Groups) actionable, and ignite their talent pipeline, because we all, at every level, crave human connection. We all want to feel like we belong inside our company.

Since that rainy Tuesday morning, stuck in my car without an umbrella, I've taken a different approach. I've given up trying to know and do it all. I acknowledged that it is okay to admit when I am exhausted, overwhelmed, burned out. I admitted the stories I write in my head about why and where I am stuck are not truths I have to live by. I realized I had a lot to learn from others. I knew I needed process-driven professional development to take charge of my career. I needed to own my part in the story I was writing.

When I started the company EDGE Leadership in 2013, I wanted to create space for the development that so profoundly transformed me to begin to transform others. Often, what we think is an individual experience, story, or challenge is really a part of a collective. What I am facing, others are facing or have faced—two or three states away or in a cubicle right down the hall. The PEER Group Coaching Framework I developed isn't only a vehicle for knowledge transfer. Through sharing and vulnerability, it empowers real change and transformation.

My experience with PEER Group Coaching was amazing! I really did not expect to have the experience that I had. In my mind, I thought I would learn some new skills, new practices, and things I could implement into my personal and professional life. But I was unaware of how deep I was going to go. It was incredible to be seen, to be validated and recognized for who I was as a person, a woman, and a woman of color, specifically as a Black woman. I don't recall having many experiences throughout all my years of education, self-development, and professional development where I felt seen, validated, and recognized as I did with the peer coaching and within my EDGE cohort. It was essential to my growth and changed my perspective of my life. It really was a life-changing experience.

—April N. Jackson,
Freelance Consultant, Coach, Educator,
Mecka Fitness and Nutrition

THE PEER REVOLUTION

I never want to diminish 1:1 Coaching. It is the gold standard. But what we know now is that generations are shifting. We now have a growing number of Millennials, like myself, who are in leadership positions and have grown up in collaborative school and social environments. We often don't expect or enjoy working alone. We want to collaborate and work with others.

The truth is, there is a tangible shift in workplace expectations in modern business culture. Instead of talking *at* me, we Millennials want to be engaged, to co-create the agenda with a focus on what's relevant for each person in this exact moment of time as it relates to where *we* want to take our career and our life. We don't want competition; we want community. But the modern workplace isn't only made up of Millennials.

In fact, there's a disparity in the workplace today. On one side, a large population of people is preparing for retirement. On the other side, a larger population of people is just getting started in their careers. While the Boomer generation peaked at sixty-seven million people, their numbers are declining every day in our workforce. In contrast, the Millennial generation, at around eighty million, is the largest generation our country has ever seen. And behind us, Gen Z is coming in fast and furious at about seventy-two million.

Like Michelle's energy company, because of this experience imbalance, companies are having to pipeline younger leaders before they are really ready—promote them before they have the experience or know-how under their belts to successfully hold leadership positions. This is exactly why, even though I was a good salesperson at Johnson and Johnson, I did not make a good sales manager at Bayer.

Gone are the days of formal mentoring programs with executives who just need to check a box, or ineffective PowerPoint driven training classes. Now is the time for innovative development frameworks that use unique, collaborative learning styles to teach what people need to know, when they need to know it, and in a way that maximizes and magnifies human potential in an organic, intentional way.

> *"There's just no denying that when people work cooperatively, great things happen."*

There's just no denying that when people work cooperatively, great things happen. That is the powerful shift that group coaching brings when done well. Yes, each person is on a personal development journey, but everyone is going through a collective journey together. Along the way, each person has something valuable to offer, something meaningful and impactful to contribute to illuminate the world as a whole. The glow from one flame may burn bright, but the glow that comes from the collective flames of many is expansive and compounding. And, most importantly, in a room full of light, we no longer feel alone.

The world is changing. People want to know they don't have to face their challenges on their own. As humans, we weren't built to go through life alone. For thousands of years, we lived in tribes, villages, outposts on the prairie where we relied on one another. In a similar way, developmental cohorts within the PEER Group Coaching Framework help elevate the human experience, maximize human potential, and raise the level of success through collaborative thinking. It's no longer about individual achievement and success, but lifting each other up, walking through the experience together, shoulder to shoulder, back to back. As human beings, we crave this type of genuine connection and belonging.

As we look to the future of coaching, a shift needs to take place to work in conjunction with the old model. It's about working together towards a supportive and collective leadership goal. 1:1 Coaching in and of itself is no longer enough. Neither, for that matter, is traditional group coaching.

PEER GROUP COACHING OPTIONS

NAME	LENGTH	GROUP SIZE
IGNITE COACHING CIRCLES	1–2 HOURS	250+
JUMPSTART	2–DAY	75–100+
THRIVE	7–MONTH	21–30+
EDGE	9–MONTH	100+

* Group size depends on organizational outcomes.

When it comes to the PEER Technology® Group Coaching Framework, equity and inclusion are the name of the game. Long gone are the days when companies seek uniformity in their talent and practices. In fact, most companies are now expected to equitably create an inclusive culture—an authentic space that curates belonging. Whether focusing on a specific group or general group that includes diverse people, the spotlight is not on one person, but on the people, the whole.

The PEER Technology® Group Coaching Framework is typically carried out in what we call our flagship EDGE experience (9 months). We do offer a THRIVE experience (7 months), and concentrated sessions such as our Ignite Coaching Circles (1-2 hours) or Jumpstart (2 days).

No matter the length of time invested, all engage the same six core elements:

THE PEER GROUP COACHING FRAMEWORK

1. The Container

Accredited coaches today are trained to coach 1:1, offering a safe space for the coachee to be vulnerable and share challenges. Coaches can then ask thoughtful questions so the coachee can generate their own solutions (and sometimes receive guidance from someone who has been there, done that). This core concept doesn't change with group coaching, but instead of the coach being the mirror that reflects back the learning, the peer group as a whole steps up to play that role. For that to occur, however, a Container must be built to provide psychological safety so the group can indeed become a group, instead of a few dozen individual spotlights, each shining in its own direction. The Container provides an environment that nurtures *vulnerability*, *intimacy*, and *relationships*.

> "Group coaching, by definition, is an ongoing experience with multiple people that supports change over time."

2. Self-Awareness

When you imagine a group coaching experience, you might picture a set of individuals, each on a personal development journey. But the truth is, they are all on that journey together. The struggles might be individual, but no one is solving them alone. Sharing individual challenges, and inviting others into this vulnerability, provides a superstructure of support and empathy for the whole. Group coaching, by definition, is an ongoing experience with multiple people that supports change over time. Self-Awareness begets more Self-Awareness. It takes courage for someone to really look at how they are showing up (and getting in their own way) and identifying where they want to go next. This Self-Awareness creates a conscious engagement within the group, which in turn cultivates more empathetic and effective leaders.

3. Outcomes

While an individual person typically determines where they are stuck and what they envision for the future while taking part in 1:1 Coaching, group coaching is different. Because every group is unique, the Framework should include reflection space to support identifying both cohort and individual Outcomes for the experience, and to create a path of accountability that leads to empowerment and transformation. These Outcomes can be shared 1:1 with the coach and with the peer group. The coach can also leverage these Outcomes in the design of the overarching experience as it relates to content and development.

4. Relevant Content

Successful group coaching isn't just about vulnerability. It's about taking that vulnerability and applying it to Relevant Content that people can sink their teeth into—content with an application they can use. This creates a support network, a web of accountability, whether to move mountains and progress higher on the career path, or simply build breadth and depth in a particular area. What is the content, you ask? That depends on the group's needs and the Outcomes they and their organization set.

5. The Practice Arena

People need a space to contribute and share best practices. This is peer mentoring—and horizontal knowledge transfer—at its finest. I use the Mastermind, a brilliantly simple peer-learning vehicle with a three-step focus: Success, Challenge, and Request for Support. Creating an intentional developmental space for vulnerability is, in essence, about creating a vehicle where people can lean on one another to contribute and be contributed to by their peers. They develop from one another's experience and lessons learned.

6. 1:1 Coaching

Coaching one another is the actionable application of learning. It is practicing vulnerability, being able to recognize and name emotions and their impact. It is what is at the heart of curating belonging because it requires a person to look at how they are holding themself back and holds them accountable to shift their choices. 1:1 Coaching is still very much needed inside every group coaching experience. As I've said, it is the gold standard. Only now, the responsibility doesn't have to be yours alone.

The International Coaching Federation definition of 1:1 Coaching is elegantly simple: *partnering with clients in a thought-provoking and creative process that inspires them to maximize their personal and professional growth.* Group coaching is amplifying that by creating the space for each and every person to learn how to become a coach to their peers. Each cohort member gives (and receives) 1:1 Coaching throughout the span of the experience. It's about creating relationships and developing intimacy that can open up possibilities far beyond what an individual could dream.

That rainy morning fifteen years ago, complete with a drenched suit jacket and frizzy, wet hair, taught me something I'll never forget—a network of supportive peer relationships is vital.

"I committed from that day forward to make sure as many people as possible realized they never have to grow alone."

It would have been easy to let that day defeat me, but even at my version of rock bottom, I knew I had to get it together, dig deep, and pull off the presentation to prove my credibility with my peers.

So I dried off my suit jacket (using the hand dryer in the bathroom!), pulled my hair off my face in a sleek, low ponytail, and focused on what matters most. I trusted in my knowledge and the opportunity I had prepared for—and I.Killed.It.

I committed from that day forward to make sure as many people as possible realized they never have to grow alone. That's the power of connection. The power of contribution. That power is there all along, within every person, a flame waiting to be ignited. The PEER group acts as a mirror, reflecting and expanding the light we each shine. The more mirrors we have around us, the brighter everything becomes.

The power of my first peer group lit my candle, and now I invite you to let me light yours.

IGNITE: BEST PRACTICES

✓ The PEER Group Coaching Framework empowers real change, accountability, and transformation. It isn't just a vehicle for knowledge transfer.

✓ Millennials and Gen Z want to be engaged in their learning and development. There is a tangible shift in workplace expectations in modern business culture. We want to co-create the agenda with a relevant focus. We don't want competition; we want community.

✓ Now is the time for innovative training frameworks that use unique, collaborative learning styles to teach what people need to know, when they need to know it, and in a way that maximizes and magnifies human potential in an organic, intentional way.

✓ Every person is on a personal development journey, and in group coaching, everyone is going through a collective journey together. Everyone has something valuable to offer, something meaningful and impactful to contribute to illuminate the world as a whole.

✓ A shift needs to take place to work in conjunction with the old models of coaching. 1:1 Coaching in and of itself is no longer enough.

✓ The PEER Technology® Group Coaching Framework is typically carried out in what we call our EDGE experience (9 months). We do offer a THRIVE experience (7 months), and concentrated Coaching Circles such as our Ignite (1-2 hours) or Jumpstart (2 days) experiences.

THOUGHT SPARKS

1. *How well equipped are you to coach and work with Millennials and Gen Z or organizations with a shifting workforce? Why does this interest you right now?*

2. *What do you enjoy most about 1:1 Coaching? In what ways do you feel your 1:1 Coaching could be more effective?*

3. *How does your current coaching and development model offer time for people to reflect on and practice new skills learned? How do you layer in real-time accountability?*

3

CHALLENGING THE SCRIPT

*"When we were children, we used to think
that when we were grown-up we would no
longer be vulnerable. But to grow up is to accept
vulnerability. To be alive is to be vulnerable."*

— MADELEINE L'ENGLE

Our job as coaches is to rekindle the flame that is always there inside each person but can occasionally get hidden from view, or worse, snuffed out entirely. We rekindle the flame of a human spirit by making connections that matter to *that* person. Our job is to help uncover what each flame needs to burn brightly once again. Our job is *not* to burn *for* others, but to be the mirror that *reflects* their own light back to them. We don't create the flame. If anything, we only re-ignite the power already present.

> "Our job is not to burn for others, but to be the mirror that reflects their own light back to them."

In my experience with 1:1 Coaching over the last two decades, the pressure is on the coach to be the mirror, but when group coaching is done well, the space is created for the entire group to become the reflecting glass. Each person in the group links together like an amazing kaleidoscope as they choose to become a mirror for one another. As they reflect back the light, it gets magnified by members of the group in ways a single coach could never do. The result is nothing less than life-transforming. And isn't that why we do what we do?

PEER GROUP COACHING OPTIONS

NAME	LENGTH	GROUP SIZE
IGNITE COACHING CIRCLES	1–2 HOURS	250+
JUMPSTART	2–DAY	75–100+
THRIVE	7–MONTH	21–30+
EDGE	9–MONTH	100+

Perhaps another personal story will help demonstrate the simple power of this peer-based approach. When I first met Tony (not his real name), he was sixty-two. I was twenty-eight. It wasn't love at first sight. A very conservative Italian, and the founder of the highly successful company I referenced earlier, he did not have any say in my being hired. And he didn't seem to be happy about it.

Perhaps, to make a point, he kept me waiting about two weeks after my first day on the job before he even introduced himself to me. How did he do it? He summoned me to his office over the loudspeaker system in the building! *Gulp.*

When I got there, he didn't get up from his desk. I stood in the doorway and tentatively said hello. I waited until he told me to come over. Only then did he stand. With the desk still between us, I hesitantly extended my hand.

He shook it and, while still holding my hand, looked me in the eye and said, "I believe women should be at home, not here in the office." I didn't know what to say... and he was *still* holding my hand!

So I just let the words find me: "Well, sir, I look forward to shifting that perception." He burst out laughing. We sat down and began a conversation—and a relationship—that forever changed my life.

Tony will always be one of the greatest mentors I've ever had. As a parent. As a leader. As an entrepreneur. In the seven years to follow as we worked and collaborated together, we both became mirrors for one another in incredibly powerful (and unexpected) ways. I like to say we transformed those first impressions—for both of us! As a pretty conservative business owner, Tony was able to challenge his own script which then enabled us to try new development pathways in the company. Plus, I was able to flip the script about my own feeling of being isolated as I entered that VP role.

AN INSIDE JOB

More on my story in a minute, but if you are a coach, you already know there's a huge gap in organizations when it comes to knowledge transfer. Companies may be really good at bringing people in from the outside to teach leadership development, but they're not always good at tapping into what is already available to them on the inside, and transferring critical knowledge from one career level to another.

Of course, they have executives who are great leaders. When thinking about how internal knowledge transfer used to be viewed, the old mindset was to turn executives into trainers and leverage them as subject matter experts. But, everyone is an individual with certain skill sets, unique abilities, and talents. The use of Agile principles helped to break down traditional views or roles, skills, and knowledge sets. As a result, we now better understand that skills and knowledge are shared across teams. While some executives are really good at business development, building relationships, and increasing revenue, others are really good at the leadership development components, like mentoring and coaching.

The conventional mentality suggests that if someone is good at something, HR leaders and internal coaches have that person, as subject matter expert (SME), put together a PowerPoint and educate new hires or those freshly promoted in "how it's done here." However, that approach simply takes talented people away from their jobs to teach and onboard other people. It essentially asks leaders to become trainers in addition to their already overloaded day jobs. It also assumes that "how I do it" as a Millennial white woman will work equally well for a Gen X African American woman, or a nonbinary Gen Z-er. It flat out doesn't work.

Another problem I've seen is expecting someone who excels in their field to also excel in managing that field. In reality, that doesn't always pan out. For example, the skill set that makes someone a good engineer doesn't necessarily make them a good manager of engineers. As I learned first-hand, the same is true for sales and just about every other area. There can be a definite skills gap when someone tries to make their next big leap.

Maybe they were promoted above their skill level. Maybe they're used to managing individual contributors and now they're managing managers. So what happens? HR leaders either hire an external company or, if they don't have the resources to do this well, assemble the PowerPoint presentations and do their best to teach others about whatever they are supposedly the experts on. But often they simply do not fit into the trainer mold. And the company gets a gap in the transferring of critical knowledge. The result is an organizational shrug: *Well, this is the best we can do.*

> "In the PEER Group Coaching Framework, participants are the experts, not the coach"

What is that missing link? Dialogue. Connection. Contribution. Community. A sharing of insights, perspectives, feedback. What's missing is the collective wisdom that comes out of peer-centered group coaching.

Although 1:1 Coaching has its benefits, integrating a group coaching framework takes those benefits to that next level. In the PEER Group Coaching Framework, participants are the experts, not the coach. It's not about a trainer telling people what to do and change. It's about creating the space for people to learn from one another. As everyone contributes, confidence builds and transformative mindset shifts occur.

With PEER Group Coaching, you're not giving people a static, three-ring binder of cookie-cutter worksheets. Instead, the PEER Framework unlocks the inherent value already existing inside the company. By facilitating dialogue, you can now bring out the best in everyone. You create the space for people to learn from one another and share their stories. To ask their questions. To give themselves permission to be vulnerable. To tap into a greater pool for insights and information. To create intentional space for organizational knowledge transfer. To collaborate. To contribute in community. To co-create.

"The goal is not to be more of what we are today, but to position ourselves to become what we can't even imagine we might need to be tomorrow."

True group coaching, while it should follow the consistent process I'll outline in this book, is never the same twice, because the people are different from one cohort to the next. The conversations are different, even in the same company. That can be a hard thing for an organization to wrap its collective mind around. (I'll talk more about this later when I talk about sales.)

In the past, training classes, mentoring programs, and 1:1 Coaching as a stand-alone system worked to maintain the status quo. Experts came in. Benchmarks were reached. Companies thrived. But times have changed, and the social and economic climate with it. All organizations now need to be nimble as innovation disrupts markets and industries we once thought were immune from disruption. Maintaining the status quo doesn't ensure the status quo. In fact, it can mean the end of an organization or industry altogether. The goal is not to be more of what we are today, but to position ourselves to become what we can't even imagine we might need to be tomorrow.

Going into my PEER experience, I had a preconceived idea of what it would be—professional women sharing thoughts, ideas, "war stories." I was correct, but it was also so much more. The absolute most powerful and impactful part for me was learning to be vulnerable. I met so many women who were just like me, going through the same struggles, the same obstacles and challenges. I have always been taught to "lead like a man"—don't show feelings, keep insecurities to yourself, don't "act like a girl." But, once I saw others opening up, I became more comfortable doing so, and I learned how to be more vulnerable.

—Kristi Gedid,
Head of Global Legal Operations

We've all endured a global pandemic with COVID-19. Now, organizations that adopt the PEER Framework for leadership development, combined with the best of targeted 1:1 Coaching and thoughtful technical training, are light years ahead of competitors.

Don't get me wrong; there is value in each of the components: training, facilitation, and 1:1 Coaching. Training increases knowledge. Facilitation is working with the group to achieve a common goal or outcome. 1:1 Coaching challenges and inspires people to discover and achieve their full potential. Yet none of these are enough on their own. That's why, with the PEER Framework, there's a little of each to make a balanced recipe for success.

Group coaching is experiential learning at its best. According to research at Oxford Brookes University, combining 1:1 *and* group coaching generates the greatest and longest lasting impact on the overall success and development of a group. Whether you are an internal or external coach, the PEER Framework multiplies impact exponentially, both for you and the cohort members.

How do you introduce a group coaching dynamic into your 1:1 Coaching practice if you are an external coach, or into organizations that are used to the standard coaching and training model if you are an internal coach? It's not uncommon for coaches to feel intimidated about tackling this new approach. Not to worry. I'll walk you through all the components in **Section Two.** And how do you sell it to decision makers in organizations? I'll share my tips and tricks with you in **Section**

Three so you can learn from both my mistakes and successes. (Because I've had plenty of both.)

The bottom line is this PEER Group Coaching Framework will help you create more of the "aha" moments when sparks reignite and lives get transformed.

THE STORIES WE TELL

My ignition moment came in 2009 when my initial working-moms group brought me face-to-face with the reality of the story I was telling myself. That rainy Tuesday morning, when I skidded into the lobby, desperately pulled myself together, and then (thankfully) delivered an amazing presentation, my work had just begun. I thought I had seen pity in the eyes of the receptionist that day, but what I came to realize was what I thought I saw was really just part of my own perception, part of a story I was telling myself. It took my peer group interactions to reveal that to me.

You see, when I was hired, one of the things I really wanted as a single mom was flexibility in my schedule. I had been working for myself previously as an external coach with Red Zebra, and before that I had enjoyed outside sales jobs that allowed me to work from home. I wanted flexibility, but during my interview in 2006, I heard, "We're an industrial company. We need butts in seats from 7:30 AM to 4:30 PM." *Strike 1.* When we talked about salary, I didn't get what I wanted either. *Strike 2.* I wasn't crazy about either reality, but was finally told, "Christy, there is just no benchmark nationally for in-house coaching in this industry. You will literally be the first. If you are as good as you say you are, the flexibility and money will come."

What I told myself upon hearing that was, *All right, I'll bet on my own horse any day of the week. I'm going to kill it. Then I'll get the money and the flex time.* So I came in, put my head down, and started cranking out work. Because he is a great leader, my manager was generous and kind, giving positive and always thoughtful feedback that kept me working at my best. I loved it, but.... I sat there waiting. *Um, when will you show me the money?* I thought. *I'm waiting for the flex time, because you said it would come if I did the work. I'm doing great work. Can't you see?*

But it didn't come. I walked out of the office after my one-year performance review with nothing more than I had when I walked in. *I guess I wasn't good enough,* I thought. *I just haven't proven myself enough. I need to do more!* So I worked even harder to prove myself over the next six months. I was determined to see the company win a certain national HR award for our development programs—and we did! *Of course, I'm going to get a raise now, right?* But no. No raise.

Now to be honest, I was getting incredibly frustrated. I experienced an entire spectrum of negative emotions but decided to keep plugging away. But eighteen months from my hire date, I was way past irritated. I was angry.

That's how it works, isn't it? When we don't check our irritation, it becomes frustration. Over time, our frustration amplifies to anger. When we don't check our anger, it becomes fury. When we don't check our fury, it becomes resentment. You know you're in resentment when everything is the other person's fault. And that's how I was starting to feel about my manager.

If we had engaged in a candid conversation during that time, I might have said, *You know, my boss is not a man of his word. He's not a man of integrity. We had a deal, but he didn't do it. Do you know of any other companies hiring right now? I don't think this is the place for me. I can't believe I closed down my own coaching company to work for him.* And on and on.

But the worst part wasn't what I said to others; it was what I was saying to myself: *What if I've made a big mistake? What if I'm really just not good enough?*

With those questions swirling around in my head, these negative thoughts began showing up in my body language. I wouldn't make eye contact when I walked down hallways. As I sat in meetings, you could see it in how I held myself, and you could hear it in my voice. Full resentment. And as coaches, we know that if we don't check our resentment, it becomes resignation. As I slipped into resignation, nothing really mattered anymore. *I'm never going to get a raise. I'm never moving up in this company.* I very nearly gave up again and not in a healthy way.

It wasn't until I was with my working mothers peer group that the spark found me again. When I started saying those terrible things (yes I really did say them out loud) and explained why I wasn't getting what I thought I deserved, a more seasoned mom in the group asked a simple but courageous question: "What would it look like to ask your boss for what you want?"

Looking back now as a coach, it was an absolutely brilliant question, but did I ever get defensive! *Why should I have to ask for a raise?* I thought. *We had a deal! He clearly said that when I delivered results, I would get what I wanted. I just needed to prove it to him.* Since then I've learned that when I feel defensive, it's time to get curious about what's underneath it. For me, strong emotions mean there is some important truth worth exploring.

After I calmed down and thought about her question, I realized she was right. I hadn't asked. When I finally did ask him about it, he looked confused. In fact, he told me he didn't even remember the conversation! He gazed at me earnestly and said, "Christy, why haven't you brought this up over the last 18 months? How long have you been carrying this?"

Sigh. I had been ready to quit. I was prepared to leave behind the best leader I've ever had the privilege to work for—in my entire career to this day—and go someplace else and start over. But with an eleven-minute authentic conversation, I fact-checked my own story. I had failed to realize that I had a choice. I felt like the story had me tangled in it, but in fact, I was the author of that script. Here I was, in full-on resentment mode, but I was writing a story my manager was not even aware of. My challenging the script only happened because a member of my peer group served as the mirror and asked a great coaching question of me. With her question, she opened my eyes and helped me become an observer of myself.

And so, I challenged the script by rewriting the story I told myself. My story. My choices. My ending to write. I walked out of his office with six flex hours a week *and* a 25% raise! He gave me everything I wanted and more. But I had to ask.

I had spent countless hours over the course of more than a year obsessing about proving myself and brooding over the situation. I'm embarrassed about the things I said about this man who is such an amazing leader. I'm equally embarrassed about the terrible things I thought about myself in my own doubts. How on earth could I get sucked into such a negative spiral?

THE KEY: VULNERABILITY

Why did I think I wouldn't have to ask for what I wanted? Somehow I thought if I just put my head down, worked hard, and delivered results, someone would put a tiara on my head and crown me Queen. I was ready to quit my job rather than have an eleven-minute conversation, and didn't think I was culpable in any of it. That perspective only shifted when I allowed myself to become vulnerable in the peer group setting. When I was willing to share what I was truly feeling, as dark and small as it was, in a space where I felt safe to share it, another person asked a powerful question because they felt safe asking it.

The key to amplifying my own flame was vulnerability. Vulnerability both permitted and empowered it to happen. Vulnerability helped me to become fearless, and I've seen it happen so many times to others through the PEER Group Coaching experience.

Fearless. What does that word mean to you? To Keri Baldinger, Director of Procurement at Gateway Health, this word came to define the outcome of the PEER experience for her. As a child, she had been exposed to physical, emotional, and drug abuse. She thought if she didn't make any noise and behaved perfectly, there would be no problems. As a nine-year old, she tried to keep a perfect household—cooking, cleaning, and caring for her five-year-old sister—all while feeling like she was walking on broken glass. So Keri learned to make herself invisible with no voice.

As she became a successful and driven business leader, she sensed that being heard was important to her happiness. She had never invested the time to focus on understanding herself, to self-reflect on why she was the way she was. She didn't understand why she gravitated to certain types of people or constantly went around saying she was "sorry".

Then she participated in one of the opening activities at the Launch session of the extended PEER experience. It's called the *I Am History* activity. In this activity, cohort members are given the space to practice vulnerability as they explore the stories they have written about themselves. They may describe their backgrounds, family influences, or other shaping experiences, but it's up to each participant how much or how little to share, if they decide to go one step further and share them out loud.

After sensing she was in a safe space in her peer group, Keri took the opportunity to reflect on and, for the first time, wrap words around her painful childhood experiences in a professional setting. And as we coaches know, language is generative. What we speak, we see in our mind's eye. And what we see, we cannot unsee. In doing so, Keri discovered more about what made her who she is, from where she got her drive, and how her perfectionistic tendencies took root. As she dug deep over the course of the next nine months of the EDGE experience, she questioned aspects of her life and choices that she had never reflected on before. Keri made this internal journey of self-reflection on her own (coaches are not therapists), yet it was a journey inspired by what she learned within the cohort. She realized her childhood had profoundly shaped her and instilled a need to feel valued and heard, but she never made the connection to how her childhood impacted her life and career. But each and every time she shared part of her story with her cohort, she became, as she describes it, more *fearless*.

This new perspective paved the way for her to intentionally develop her leadership brand, purpose, and vision. She even applied her new fearless perspective to conduct a 1:1 Career Interview with David Holmberg, CEO of Highmark Health. This optional part of the PEER Framework gives members the opportunity to reach up and engage with top leaders. They learn from those leaders and begin to plant authentic seeds for organic mentoring and sponsorship relationships to advance their careers. When I told her cohort they could choose anyone from the company to interview, she immediately thought fearlessly and asked, *Why not the CEO?* Because she acted courageously, Keri demonstrated her personal brand to one of the most important people in the company. In addition, the experience reaffirmed why Keri chose to stay at Gateway—to be guided by an inspirational leader with a strategic direction she could embrace.

More than three years later, Keri continues to lean into this fearless approach that grew out of her being vulnerable in her group-coaching setting. Through the PEER Group Coaching experience, Keri defined what is truly important to her and why.

It helped her feel more in charge of her options. It allowed her to discover what she was willing to accept, and, just as importantly, what she was not. Not only did she get promoted then, but she has continued to advance into new positions since.

Now Keri seeks out opportunities to be fearless, to have the courage to speak up with her own voice, and to step up when perhaps others cannot or will not.

WHERE VULNERABILITY BEGINS

The PEER Group Coaching Framework pairs vulnerability with empathy, allowing a team to understand they don't have everything under control all the time. We discovered how to show our team a real connection so they can relate to each other. Letting my guard down as a leader, while difficult, creates a connection and allows the team to see we are just like them.

—Todd W. Faulk,
Vice President of Human Resources, Duquesne Light Company

The success of the PEER Group Coaching Framework depends on the level of vulnerability. People need to be willing to reflect on and challenge their stories (and the critical role they play in writing them). Only when they challenge those stories, can they rewrite them. And only when they get vulnerable, can they be willing and able to authentically rewrite them with genuine self-awareness.

Guess what coaches? Vulnerability starts with us. As I've learned over the last twenty years of coaching, and as you have no doubt observed in your own coaching experiences, we cannot coach others to be vulnerable if we are not willing to be vulnerable ourselves.

I needed to give myself permission to be vulnerable, to be willing to share my deep frustrations and my negative inner self-talk at the time that was eroding my confidence and my productivity. Only when I said it out loud and declared it could I get the perspective I needed to see things differently. I could only observe myself in the mirror when someone I respected and trusted held it up for my own personal and professional development. Vulnerability opened the door for progress and growth. And that's how it works every time.

As coaches, we must both model vulnerability and amplify it. Vulnerability is the wick of the collective candle, if you will. Without it, there can be no fueling of the flames, no igniting of potential. When we model vulnerability to the group, we give them permission to be vulnerable themselves. Vulnerability begets vulnerability. As Brené Brown says, "Vulnerability feels like fear but looks like courage." In addition, her research demonstrates that courage is contagious.

Yet everyone, every generation, at every business level, struggles with being vulnerable. Often, the lack of confidence holds people back. Their story about "not being good enough" keeps them from going for the promotion, setting healthy boundaries, dreaming big. As a result, people tend to think they shouldn't advocate for themselves, because it could sound like bragging or complaining. I have found that women especially struggle with this reality. Many of us were taught, often at our mother's knee, that it is not nice to brag. We're told that being "boastful" makes others feel "less than." So, we learn to keep our successes private and, even if we do share them, we often downplay their significance.

There is a very real cost to that limiting mindset, both to individuals and to organizations. As an individual, it can cost in terms of career mobility and life fulfillment. In organizations, when we don't create the intentional space of celebrating and acknowledging who is really good at what—folks simply don't know who in their network they can learn from to succeed when confronted by similar challenges. Everyone ends up repeatedly reinventing the wheel. There may be hundreds or even thousands of people in an organization struggling with what they think is an individual challenge that is actually part of a collective experience—they just lack the vehicle through which to learn how to solve it. Withholding successes actually prevents people from sharing important insights with others. They lose innovation. Creativity. Progress.

All of it requires a degree of vulnerability that simply is not found in most corporate settings. When it comes right down to it, vulnerability is the fuel that feeds the flames of successful group coaching. As we coaches know, especially if we are coaching in Western cultures, it often does not come naturally. Consequently, the process and environment must be crafted intentionally. I'll show you how to do that in Section Two, because it is worth it.

People rarely choose to walk alone on the career and life journey. More often than not, they simply get so busy they forget to invest in personal relationships at home and at work. The unfortunate and unintentional consequence is that they limit themselves and others. When someone hides their light under a bushel, not only can they no longer see what's directly in front of them, but no one else can benefit

"The beauty of peer mentoring is that in a room full of light, people no longer feel alone."

from the radiance. The beauty of peer mentoring is that in a room full of light, people no longer feel alone. They finally give themselves permission to shine.

To understand how each person can let their light shine, and how you as a coach can use the PEER Framework to ignite the potential in others, you'll first need to understand the nature of the journey up the Growth Mountain and why having illumination along the way is so important.

IGNITE: BEST PRACTICES

✓ The goal is not to be more of what we are today, but to position ourselves to become what we can't even imagine we might need to be tomorrow.

✓ Our job is to help uncover what everyone's flame needs to burn brightly. Our job is *not* to burn *for* others, but to be the mirror that *reflects* their own light back to them.

✓ The PEER Group Coaching Framework fosters dialogue, connection, contribution, and community. This sharing of insights, perspectives, and feedback offers a collective wisdom that improves both personal and professional Outcomes.

✓ Integrating a group coaching framework takes the benefits of 1:1 Coaching to the next level. In the PEER Group Coaching Framework, participants are the experts, not the coach. As everyone contributes, confidence builds and transformative mindset shifts occur.

✓ Vulnerability starts with us as the Group Coach. The key to amplifying my own flame was vulnerability. We cannot coach others to be vulnerable if we are not willing to be vulnerable ourselves.

✓ Withholding successes actually prevents people from sharing important insights with others. They lose innovation, creativity, and progress.

THOUGHT SPARKS

1. How effectively does your coaching help people challenge and rewrite the scripts to their stories? What works well? What doesn't?

2. Where do you feel vulnerable in your coaching practice right now? Why does this feel urgent to address?

3. What do you see in the PEER Framework that is missing from your current approach?

4. What does the status quo look like in your practice or organization or team? What is the cost of staying where you are?

4

THE GROWTH MOUNTAIN

"Our deepest fear is not that we are inadequate. Our deepest fear is that we are powerful beyond measure."

— MARIANNE WILLIAMSON

It may help to imagine the people you group coach in an organization as taking a journey on a Career Growth Mountain. Think of how most of us get started on our professional journey. When we start out in our career, it's like we start off in the field at the foot of the Mountain. In this Early Career Field, there are gorgeous wildflowers, cute animals, curiosities, and lots to explore. There are also dangers. Sinkholes we don't know are there until we walk into them and fall. Dangerous coyotes that are on the prowl for naive prey.

As we move through our career, we often want to continue to amplify our visibility and competence. We yearn to see sights other than the fields. We start to climb and move into more of a wooded, forested area near the base of the Mountain. As anyone who has ever explored the forest knows well, the experience can vary and will look different for different people.

In these woods, we find new things to explore that couldn't exist in the fields—gorgeous waterfalls and streams, new varieties of trees, and verdant landscapes. We discover beautiful foliage and wide-ranging temperatures, from the north to south-facing sides of the Mountain. We find new dangers here, too. We might come upon a cave with a family of bears inside. We might see plentiful and gorgeous red berries, but only after we eat them do we discover they are poisonous.

Some people may happily choose to spend their entire career in this forest area, what I would refer to as Mid-Career Woods. Some folks try their hand at managing others and leave the life of an individual contributor behind, building campfires of connection and teaching new recruits how to live off the land. Others build and develop breadth and depth of expertise with the wildlife in the pine cove, or become a subject matter expert in their passion area by focusing on a disease spreading amongst the willows by the eastern stream.

Still others feel the tug to keep climbing, and start moving up into the rocky, craggy area above the treetops. There, the vegetation is scarce. On any given day, they may meet a friendly old mountain goat or a clever mountain lion lying in wait for dinner. Because there are fewer people at this height on the Mountain, it can start to feel lonelier, a feeling compounded by the fact that they may be more exposed than ever before. The wind whips constantly. The sun burns. But it is only at this level that they can see the beauty of the breathtaking vistas.

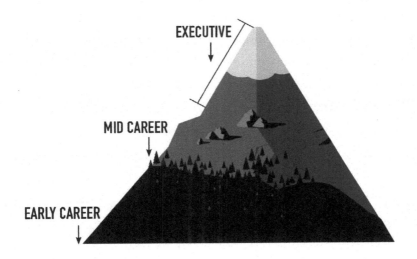

EXECUTIVE

MID CAREER

EARLY CAREER

Depending on the size of the organization, we might think of this area near the top of the Career Growth Mountain as the domain of the VPs and Officers of a company. Just below where the vegetation wanes would be the Managing Directors (MD) whose role is to manage everyone in the Mid-Career Woods - who, in turn, lead the individual SMEs and early career individual contributors who are often newer to the Mountain. From the rocky crags above the treetops, MDs and VPs can see smoke billowing from the Early Career Fields and large crowds gathering on the ridge in the distance, but cannot tell why. Are they angry? Are they celebrating? Maybe they can hear a ruckus in the foliage of the Woods below, but can't see through the thick vegetation to know what is causing it.

Meanwhile, all the way at the top of the Mountain, sits the CEO. At that altitude, there are dangers folks on the rest of the

Mountain haven't even imagined, but the view is unparalleled. Sometimes the air gets so thin they have to wear an oxygen pack. And the CEO is always alone. They no longer have peers inside the organization. Their peers sit atop their own Mountains many miles away. The CEO can still benefit from their experiences, but can't exactly walk down the trail to make meaningful connections like those that take place in the forest.

> My PEER experience showed me ways to counsel, motivate, teach, coach, and mentor my subordinates and my peers. It also taught me ways to develop communication paths with my superiors. With the peer group and peer discussions, I was able to learn what others at each level were doing to develop themselves and to become better leaders. Great experience. Great learning curve, and a great way to develop my future.
>
> **—Paul Walker,**
> *Consol Energy*

I have tested and refined the PEER Framework in Fortune 500 companies with people at every level of the Career Growth Mountain. Creating peer groups in the Early Career Field, in the rocky, craggy area of MDs, officers, and VPs, and most definitely in the Mid-Career Woods. In fact, as of this writing, our team of coaches has engaged more than 10,000 mid-career leaders alone. Within group coaching, I've found that the Growth Mountain concept helps connect dots most of us didn't even know were there, making the invisible visible. It's what an organization doesn't even know it needs, because until now there simply hasn't been a consistent way to leverage knowledge transfer amongst peers.

Inside a Mid-Career group coaching cohort, for example, everyone may be in the woods together, but likely they're all on different parts of the Mountain. They can learn from one another. Don't touch the berry bushes on the southern-facing side, because they will make you sick for days. Those who have lived here longer can tell you that the bears that used to live in that cave by the waterfall have moved out. Now it is a good space to wait out a storm. This horizontal knowledge transfer is a game-changer.

But so is the vertical knowledge transfer that can take place between Mountain levels as a result of the PEER Framework. As we saw with Keri in the last chapter, she got to engage firsthand with the CEO. Not only did she learn a lot from that experience, but the CEO also asked questions, perhaps discovering more about that organizational smoke he saw in the distance. That one interaction is a microcosm of the horizontal and vertical knowledge benefits and gets multiplied many times over for an organization using the PEER Framework.

In my experience, the PEER Group Coaching Framework allows people to navigate the Career Growth Mountain to find greater fulfillment and success in their work lives, but the analogy can shift to whatever life domain is relevant for anyone. For that reason, this Growth Mountain analogy could just as easily be called whatever you choose to focus your coaching practice on. The Framework is just as effective for a middle manager in a Fortune 100 company as it is for a peer group of entrepreneurs who, like my group of working mothers, may have a rich diversity of experience. Some may be in the Early Stage Field, while others are in the Scaling the Business Woods. Or a group of parents of transgender kids, where so many of us began in the Field of Shock and Awe, may be traveling up to the Settling into Our New Reality Woods. The process is exactly the same. As a coach, you naturally want to find out where people are on their Mountain trek and what developmental space they are in, so you can help create the space for the connections that matter most to them right now.

Some Growth Mountains are the organizations in which a person works, their internal strategic network. Others may be content with their relationships on their Organizational Mountain, but want to increase their credibility and visibility in their industry or field. In this case, their desired Mountain trek is external to their company. Perhaps they want to represent their company at a conference or sit on a panel and share their expertise. For still others, the Growth Mountain may be their community. They want to sit on a non-profit board and need to build an intentional strategic network to do so. And there is always the Personal Life Mountain everyone must navigate, where the weather is always shifting around marriage, parenthood, and friendships. Others want to move, going from the

Mountain they know and completely starting over. In my experience, people often have the most success when they are able to truly focus on any one Growth Mountain at a time. These possible group coaching areas, and what people need in each of them, is always evolving as they experience real life together.

THE GROWTH MOUNTAIN PRISM

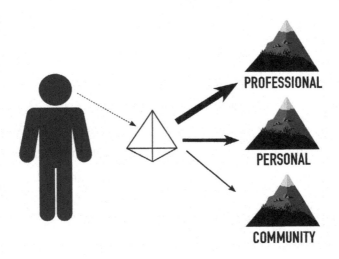

Whatever the area, the questions to help someone see through the personal prism and choose the emphasis that works for them remain the same: Do they want to climb higher, or are they content for now where they are? Where are they feeling inadequate? What do they need to move them forward? Do they want to stay on this Mountain, or explore another? Some folks will reinvent themselves three, four, or even five times across their career, starting each time at the base of a different

Growth Mountain. The analyst living in a treehouse in the woods becomes a brand-new nurse at the base of a larger Mountain farther north. The VP of sales, who used to sit and strategize on the rocky cliffs at sunset, becomes an entrepreneur, deep in the execution weeds as a consultant and vendor to the company where they once led. In my case, I was an executive coach who became an HR leader who became a group coach. The single person gets married or the middle-aged person finds themselves suddenly divorced and back in the Dating Field for the first time in seventeen years.

"Group coaching is all about experiential learning, applying learning to life."

The answers to those questions will affect how a productive, safe space for growth gets created within the PEER Group Coaching Framework. After all, group coaching is all about experiential learning, applying learning to life.

For the individual, utilizing the PEER Group Coaching Framework on their choice of Growth Mountain is like taking an old school map out from the glove compartment and converting it to a 3D GPS app, complete with traffic notifications and "just in time" rerouting. It improves personal, strategic planning, helps participants chart their chosen career path, and understand what, when, and how to leverage resources—and when and how to *be* those resources to others.

At the organizational level, domains may form around EBRGs or other actionable networks (LGBTQ+, leaders of African ancestry, women, men leading inclusive organizations, etc.). On the other hand, domains may form around key talent groups, such as managing directors, senior managers, early career engineers, front line leaders—the possibilities are endless, depending on the organizational needs.

THE THREE LENSES

The PEER Group Coaching Framework uses three lenses to ignite the flames of success and achievement throughout the Mountain trek—mentoring, coaching, and advocacy. We'll reference these terms throughout the pages to come, but these three key growth lenses often get confused because they have a lot in common. They are all about maximizing people's potential, but they each do it from a different perspective. No matter which lens we look through, knowledge and opportunity always get transferred down from those with more experience and expertise. In return, feedback and perspective travel upwards. But that doesn't always mean mentors must be higher up the Mountain than we are. Or that advocates can't be at the same level beside you.

First, *mentoring* is an unequal power relationship between two individuals—one with significant domain experience and the other a learner, ready to take in new information. It is a misnomer that mentors need to be older than us. I am being mentored right now by a twenty-three-year-old on TikTok. A mentor is simply someone who has more domain experience than someone else in a particular area of the Growth Mountain that we want to learn how to navigate. It's an imbalanced relationship where the power is truly in the person who has the knowledge. As the mentor shares stories, experiences, and best practices, the mentee gains insights from someone who has been there, done that. The mentor often gives advice, or even flat out tells someone what they think should be done.

But sometimes mentoring can miss the mark, like when what a mentor says doesn't land well. For example, a Black woman in her late twenties may not relate to the older, white male mentor telling her what he would do. Truth be told, sometimes I listen to mentors, and sometimes I don't. Sometimes their stories bring incredible insight and value, and sometimes they are outdated (if I happen to know, for example, that the bears they are cautioning me about actually no longer live in that cave by the waterfall). This is where coaches can give a fresh and needed perspective.

Unlike mentoring, *coaching* is an equal power relationship. Coaches don't tell someone what to do. Instead, they ask thoughtful questions that empower the coachees to generate their own solutions. Coaching is about creating capacity inside other human beings to critically think through their own issues. Coaches don't simply give advice or presume to have the answers. We are not problem solvers. We simply offer support, accountability, and companion people on their way.

The truth is, everybody's best solution always comes from themselves. No one knows and understands a challenge or unique situation like the individual person. But what we all struggle with (now, more than ever) is finding the space to work through challenges, as you saw clearly in my opening story. The PEER Group Coaching experience takes this concept to the next level by not relying on the group coach to be the only coach in the room. Instead, it teaches people how to become coaches, not only for others, but also for themselves, and provides a safe space to practice the coaching skills they can then take back to their little enclave on their Growth Mountain. It intentionally creates an environment that encourages practicing vulnerability, building relationships, and developing the transferable coaching skills they can immediately put into play in all kinds of places and spaces—both at work and at home.

"The truth is, everybody's best solution always comes from themselves. No one knows and understands a challenge or unique situation like the individual person."

Yet, that is still not enough. There needs to be the third lens of *advocacy*. Advocates, like mentors, also have an unequal power relationship. The difference is what's transferred from the mentor to the mentee is knowledge. What's transferred from an advocate to the person they are sponsoring is opportunity. People need advocates to bring up their names when they themselves are not in the room. Advocates are the folks who bring opportunities to others, who know what they're good at and, just as importantly, where they want to go next on their Growth Mountain. Advocates speak up on another person's behalf. When I coach high-potential managers inside the Mid-Career Woods inside large organizations, I advise them that their best advocate is likely someone two levels above them in that rocky, craggy area on the Mountain in their organization. The best advocate needs to be at a higher level of visibility to see opportunities they cannot see from deep within the folds of the forest, like the dangers from a coming avalanche.

Mentors and coaches want to see people succeed. We mentor or coach because we want to give back after someone has done that for us. It feels good to mentor other people. I genuinely do not look for my mentees to give anything back to me. I pour into them because I feel good (and competent, to be honest) at the end of a mentoring session.

Advocates are similar, but also very different. There is an unspoken quid pro quo, in fact. Every advocate is looking for two specific things from the relationship. If they are not met, the relationship will usually not continue. The first is pretty obvious: if the recipient does not deliver, the advocate will not continue to advocate for them. If I am lending my name and credibility on someone's behalf, I expect them to walk in and kick butt. The second thing is what often gets missed. Advocates are looking for valuable feedback and perspective to better achieve *their* strategic goals.

AN ADVOCATE EXAMPLE

Perhaps the best way to explain how advocates work is through a story. When I was in my early thirties, I wanted to focus on my Community Growth Mountain. I had settled into my role as the VP of HR and was feeling confident in my internal Career Growth Mountain. We were winning regional and national awards for our L&D programming. I was representing my company on the national stage (the external Career Growth Mountain). My personal life felt settled, so it was time to think about my community. I knew I wanted to sit on a non-profit board to enhance my leadership capability, but also knew that wasn't going to just happen. I needed to leverage my network.

After I shared my interest with some folks in my external career network, they offered me a chance to serve on a committee for a large nonprofit. It was there that I met Laura Ellsworth. Laura was a Partner-in-charge of a large law firm, Jones Day, and is a total powerhouse in my local community of Pittsburgh. I admit, I had a bit of a girl crush on her from afar, but then I put my head down and went to work, bringing value to the committee in any way I could. Within six months, more opportunities started coming my way, like speaking at a large regional event, serving on two more committees, and finally, after one year, the invitation to sit on my first non-profit board.

I then started getting curious about how these opportunities were finding me. As it turned out, they all came through someone who had been advocating for me—Laura Ellsworth.

As a student of leadership development, I knew if I wanted these opportunities to continue, I needed to start bringing value to her in the form of feedback and perspective. When I thought about where Laura was on the Community Growth Mountain, I understood she was right near the tip top, while I was brand-new to the forest. Her job was to look out into the future of the Pittsburgh region and beyond and think big and strategically. So I asked her what *her* goals were, then offered insights that could help her achieve them. From my unique vantage point, I could offer what Laura herself could no longer see and give a fresh perspective from within the forest. I could leverage my personal connections in the fields and give detailed explanations as to why those crowds were gathering on that faraway ridge. Although power dynamics in relationships exist, value always transcends it. We all learn from one another regardless of where we are presently camping on any given Mountain.

As a result, our relationship blossomed in ways I could never have imagined. Five years later, when a national nonprofit asked Laura to serve as Chair, she declined, but she suggested they talk with me. That Chair seat ultimately led to the opportunity to sit on my first for-profit board a few years

> *"Mountains, like people, are never alone. They always exist within the context of a range."*

later, which catapulted me to new heights on my External Career Mountain because our Mountains are always connected. Always. Because mountains, like people, are never alone. They always exist within the context of a range.

These three lenses—mentoring, coaching, and advocacy— each play a key role within the PEER Group Coaching Framework. Participants can learn how to leverage each of these roles outside of the cohort to achieve their goals, like my example with Laura. They can also look to their peers for mentorship— those with the experience and wisdom from a different area of the Mountain, yet within the same field or demographic. When they share a challenge and ask for help from a peer mentoring standpoint, they are sharing with people who they trust will offer the advice they need. They then can also benefit from peer advocates who share their successes with a network outside of their own.

But mentorship and advocacy can only go so far. That is where coaches come in. The lens of coaching in the PEER Framework brings together people from the same level on the

Mountain, so the entire group becomes coaches for one another. We always involve 1:1 Coaching in the Framework as we teach and equip everyone to be a coach, because often the best coaches, the ones who empathize the most, are peers who are at or near the same spot on the desired Growth Mountain.

THE POWER OF INTENTIONAL RELATIONSHIPS

Christine McAnlis had been in a male-dominated industry for her entire career. She started out with an electrical engineering major, then went straight into software development and worked at a highly-competitive company for eighteen years.

She always felt as though she had to do twice as well as some of the men she worked with just to say that she was working as hard. As a collaborative person, networking enabled her to succeed at a highly-competitive company. But Christine was stopping herself from taking any next steps because she had been focusing on only what was in front of her, instead of taking the time to determine what she wanted. She needed to realize her next move and formulate a plan to get there.

I met Christine after she had transitioned to her current career in IT, where she was in the midst of desperately trying to prove herself as one of the only women and show her unique value. But by going through our 2-day Jumpstart group coaching experience, Christine learned she was not alone in her struggles.

One of her most significant takeaways was understanding the distinction between coaches, mentors, and advocates. In just twelve short hours, she learned to serve in each of these roles and allowed herself to receive perspectives from each of them in her own life as well. She began to see how she could become a better advocate for others and how to become a better mentor to others she was already mentoring.

As she listened to the organization's executives serving as Guest Mentors sharing insights (vertical knowledge transfer) in the PEER Jumpstart experience, she learned more about the power of intentionally building strategic relationships across her Growth Mountain range. Like many women, she had always been naturally good at creating relationships, but not always in an intentional way that would help her achieve her career and life goals. She learned that simply creating them wasn't enough. She had to practice leveraging them.

This journey of self-discovery, while only for two days, powerfully shifted possibilities for Christine. She left that second day with an accountability group of peer coaches to support her as she executed her plan to stop apologizing, own who she was, and understand her goals.

She stopped making excuses for others who were doing the bare minimum to get by, and quietly, but firmly, started holding them accountable using coaching techniques. Christine decided to be big and bold by interviewing for and receiving a promotion to become a manager at a major bank. She went from a very small mountainside where she was doing really well to the forest area of a much larger Mountain. However, she now has a secret weapon: the confidence gained from the PEER Group Coaching experience and the relationships she has intentionally cultivated because of it. One year after that PEER experience, Christine still maintains monthly meetings with her Jumpstart cohort accountability group and intentionally manages her relationships with sponsors, mentors, and advocates in her life.

Mentorship, coaching, advocacy—when they all work in harmony, it's a beautiful thing, but first, it is important to know how to bring them all together.

IGNITE BEST PRACTICES

✓ In the Early Career Field, when we start out in a career or when we reinvent ourselves in a substantial way, it's like starting off in the field at the foot of the Growth Mountain. In this Field, we often want to continue to amplify our visibility and competence.

✓ The Mid-Career Woods offers people the experience of spending time in the forest area of the Growth Mountain. Some try their hand at managing others, some build campfires of connection and teach, others become subject matter experts in their passion areas.

✓ Certain individuals feel the tug to keep climbing and start moving up into the rocky, craggy area above the treetops. This area is near the top of the Growth Mountain and is the domain of VPs and officers of a company.

✓ The Growth Mountain concept helps make visible what an organization doesn't even know it needs. The vertical knowledge transfer between Mountain levels is a consistent addition to amplify the horizontal knowledge transfer that occurs amongst peers.

✓ The PEER coaching framework uses three lenses to ignite the flames of success and achievement throughout the Mountain trek: mentoring, coaching, and advocacy.

✓ The PEER Group Coaching experience teaches people how to become coaches for themselves, and provides a safe space to practice the coaching skills they can then take back to their little enclave on the Mountain.

THOUGHT SPARKS

1. As you reflect on your own career, how do the different stages resemble the Growth Mountain? Internally inside your organization? Outside in your field and industry? In your community?

2. From your vantage point as a coach, which areas of the Growth Mountain do you think could benefit from PEER Group Coaching the most (Early Career, Mid-Career, Executive)? Why?

3. *How effectively do you see vertical knowledge transfer happening in your organization or between those you coach right now? What factors prevent this transfer from happening well?*

4. *Do you think organizations today tend to focus more on mentoring, coaching, or advocacy? Why?*

5

PEER COACHING IN ACTION

"Your visions will become clear only when
you can look into your own heart. Who looks
outside, dreams; who looks inside, awakes."

— CARL JUNG

Before we unpack each of the six Elements in the PEER Group Coaching process in detail, it may help to see a 15,000-foot view of the process as it unfolded in a real world setting.

Sheetz is a family-owned and operated convenience store chain based in Altoona, PA. We began working with them in the midst of the COVID-19 pandemic, but the relationship began in the same way many of them do—after some of their leaders had taken a test drive of the PEER approach.

The PEER Group Coaching Framework really shines as an internal leadership development experience within a company that is ready for it. However, I have found that an open-enrollment, external cohort is a great place to give leaders in these organizations a chance to experience the Framework. (As a side note, this is an easy step if you want to create spaces for the concentrated, 1-2-hour Ignite Coaching Circles, because you can offer pro bono experiences relatively painlessly. Offering a 2-day Jumpstart, or even a 9-month EDGE experience, is a bit of a different story. In my experience, marketing and delivering the extended options as a public offering became way more efficient when I partnered with an organization that had a similar audience so we could share expenses and profits.)

If you recall, when I unintentionally beta tested the PEER Framework, the SWSG cohorts were women from a variety of industries and backgrounds. So we created an external cohort in 2016, in partnership with the Pittsburgh Technology Council, a membership organization, so their companies could send one or several women to participate in our extended group coaching offering. The 9-month experience, called EDGE: Education and Development through Group Experience, gives companies the opportunity to explore the value of group coaching for a minimal cost. Plus, with a public cohort, I'm also able to serve participants from small to midsize businesses who usually don't have the budget (or talent pipeline) to bring in our standard, custom 6-9 month group coaching experiences.

Sheetz sent a few women over the course of three years to this open enrollment EDGE cohort, and several others to our 2-day Jumpstart experience, both offered through our partnership with the Pittsburgh Technology Council. As a result, the subsequent sale of our group coaching products was seeded through actual experience of their leaders working with us and the PEER Framework.

Both external and internal coaches should note that easing into the relationship with a public cohort minimizes risk for both the external coach and the company. For the external coach, it provides an opportunity to ensure the company culture is ready for this innovative approach. For the company, it is an opportunity to become familiar with and verify they are comfortable with the Framework.

The bottom line is that as a result of their experiences in our public cohort, Sheetz came to me in late 2019 to find out how they could bring the 9-month EDGE experience into their company.

They wanted to increase employee engagement, retention, and mobility across a specific subset—women. Because we hear similar needs from all the clients we serve, I knew EDGE could significantly help with all of those. I was impressed with the leadership at Sheetz for seeing the need to invest specifically in their front-line women leaders.

Little did they know, a pandemic was coming that would put the focus, more than ever, on those front-line leaders. Those leaders kept Sheetz on the map. When people didn't show up for work because of quarantining or exposure, those front-line leaders often worked two shifts a day, six days a week. They might not see their families for days or weeks for fear of exposing them.

At first, like a lot of great companies, the Sheetz leadership evaluated whether the time was right to invest into a new initiative in the midst of economic uncertainty. They had never offered a targeted leadership development experience for their women before. Was the concept of group coaching too new? Was this the right level of leader on which to focus? Was this the right time? But, as they moved into summer of 2020 and other cultural events surfaced, like the death of George Floyd and the *Wall Street Journal* sounding the alarm about high numbers of women leaving the workforce due to family concerns, they made the decision to invest in their female front-line leaders.

So in the midst of a pandemic, we launched EDGE in a 100% virtual setting with twenty-four women, most of whom didn't even have a laptop or iPad. Now, I know some coaches reading this right now may have a hard time grasping how anyone could do effective group coaching with more than six or eight people (like in the Traditional Group Coaching Model below). If that's you, stay tuned, because the ideal size for EDGE is between twenty-one to thirty people. (The 2-day Jumpstart can have 75 to 100. The Ignite Coaching Circles and THRIVE can have more than 250. Think about the opportunities that can open for either your external coaching business or your internal development plans!)

TRADITIONAL GROUP COACHING

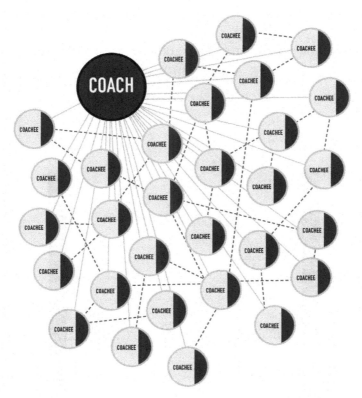

PEER GROUP COACHING
* Shading denotes that every coachee
also plays the role of coach.

The reality is, the PEER coaching framework is all about *peer learning*. When you have only a handful of people in a group, they look to the coach as more of a consultant, the expert to tell them how to do things. They can easily miss the richness of truly being able to bring value and contribute in an authentic way to one another.

Because of the pandemic and the geographic location of their leaders, the entire PEER group experience with Sheetz was done virtually. Prior to March of 2020, we had already been employing a hybrid model in which 75% of the PEER Framework was virtual, so the shift wasn't that significant for us. However, it did cause us to approach things a little differently as we began to engage the six Elements of the experience.

* Self Awareness is the filter through which everything arrives and leaves the cohort.

First, as we built the **Container**, creating a safe place for participants to share, we had to consider different factors. For example, we always consider the context: What's going on in the company? Are revenues up or down? Is a new product launch taking place? Are layoffs happening? What about the market in which they compete? Even when we do a public cohort, we need to be thoughtful about the region or nation in which the coaching is taking place.

What we learned with this Sheetz experience is that now, thanks to technology, the context in which virtual group coaching takes place is, well, the entire world. Not only was everyone experiencing a worldwide pandemic at the time, some cohort members lived or worked in cities where riots were taking place, while others did not. That meant we all had to be even more intentional about **Self-Awareness**, especially me. I'll share more about our unique approach to Self-Awareness later, but we recognized early in the process that all of these women were going on personal development journeys in the midst of some pretty unique times. Perhaps the greatest gift each of them gained from the experience was knowing they were not alone. They were part of a collective. They had peers.

As a coach, I've always preached that we have to meet people where they are. But meeting this group where they were was different, because these women (and those identifying as women) did not fit the typical corporate coaching profile. For example, most of them had no college degree and no formal post-secondary education. In my experience, until this point, I had only worked with high-potentials in organizations, not front-line leaders. What I assumed was people who have had more education or have engaged in some kind of personal development with a therapist or coach come into the group coaching experience with a higher level of Self-Awareness and can therefore better maximize the impact.

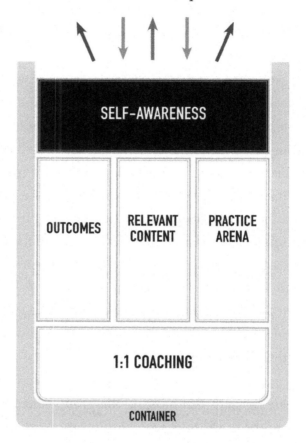

Now, I'm not even going to try to sugarcoat my bias here. To be totally candid, I came into the experience not expecting this cohort to have invested in their own personal growth or development. I assumed they would not be reading self-help books, seeing therapists, or engaging coaches. I presumed they would have a wealth of lived experiences, for sure, practical hands-on education in the real world, but that's it. I was floored by what I encountered.

Here I was thinking I was going to be planting Self-Awareness seeds that would germinate and bloom at some point in the future, but right from the initial stories shared as we built the Container, it was obvious these women were already highly self-aware. Not only did it surprise me, but it seemed to surprise and encourage the women in the cohort. We had a couple of powerful stories shared right in the Launch of the experience as part of the activities we do (Yes, I'll share those later, too) that showed me my bias had been dead wrong. Women from all walks of life—single, married, divorced, gay, straight—shared stories of intense family relational pain and career challenges, and how they had walked through it with mentors, therapists, and a high level of Self-Awareness.

When it came time to identify **Outcomes** for the group coaching experience, what we discovered was the women mostly felt alone and burnt out. That is why it is always critical to evaluate both the Outcomes desired by the company and the Outcomes desired by the people in the cohort. The PEER Group Coaching Framework is designed to do both. If I didn't achieve *their* Outcomes, we would fail, regardless of if we accomplished what the company wanted, because the fuel in group coaching comes from the peer group itself.

Identifying Outcomes is a bit like personal strategic planning. We create the space for Self-Awareness to continually unfold as the person's experience deepens. They get to continuously chart their own path. It all begins with initially identifying their Outcomes. Those Outcomes may shift based on Relevant Content they encounter in the experience, by someone's contribution in a Practice Arena, or during 1:1 Coaching. Their Outcomes are always evolving as new pathways light up for them.

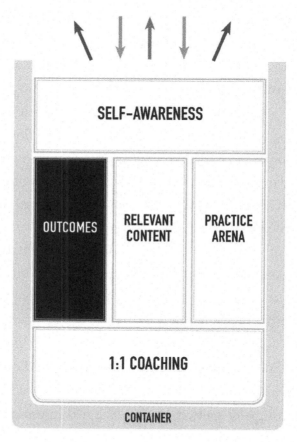

I applaud the Sheetz organization for having the courage to forge new ground. They had never focused on women's leadership development before in such an intentional way, and on top of that, they were skipping over traditional training classes designed to "fix" women leaders, and leaping right into group coaching 100% virtually! So, part of the organization's Self-Awareness was to view the PEER Framework as a way to build an internal network of coaches as their female leaders learned, then applied, the Framework. Most large companies have EBRGs, but the PEER Framework gives them a network and shared language to take action and help one another.

In fact, think of the image on the front cover of this book. (Go ahead and take a look, I'll wait.) The people in the golden coaching group circle form connections, both within and beyond the groups as a result of the experience. Those connections then empower them to shine their own lights and reflect back the lights of others. When those pathways are lit, people know they don't need to have all the answers because they now know other people who do, and who are eager to make connections on their behalf. Because a safe Container was built and cohort members have the Self-Awareness to admit what they need, they can be vulnerable and make requests for support to one another. That's where genuine growth takes place.

Coaching, influential leadership, and personal brand were the three competency areas on which the company focused their organizational Outcomes, which were based on their people analytics and data. After that was decided, we asked the cohort members themselves what other **Relevant Content** they wanted to engage with in their EDGE Experience. I worked with company HR leadership to create a menu of additional topics from which the women could choose to ensure they got to co-create their group coaching experience. Based on the individual Outcomes of the women, I focused on applying Relevant Content, first to coaching, and then on making the influential connections that mattered most to them across their Career and Life Growth Mountains.

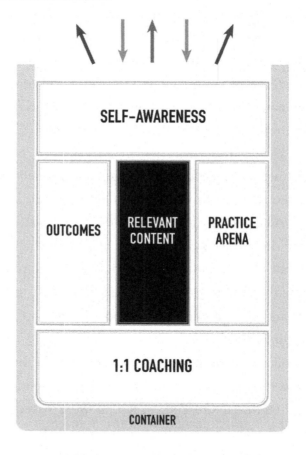

As I'll explain more in Chapter Eight, the PEER approach to Relevant Content is unique in a number of ways. Rather than bringing in outside experts, we enlist Guest Mentors, usually executives from within the organization, in ways that provide incredible value, both to cohort members and to the Guest Mentors themselves. So when our clients look inside their organization and find executive leaders passionate about the topics the cohort chooses, they begin to create a matrix of people who are authentically living those topics in their corporate culture.

These Guest Mentor experiences can also create purposeful learning spaces for the Guest Mentors themselves. For example, Sheetz wanted to build a sustainable pipeline of female talent, so why settle for impacting only the twenty-four women in the cohort? Why not think even bigger and more strategically? In creating their Guest Mentor pairs for each topic, they amplified the growth possibilities and ensured they got a bonus return on their group coaching investment. They decided to select a male C-Suite leader (we'll call him John, living up above the rocky part of the Mountain) and a female executive (we'll call her Julie, who had just moved out of the Mid-Career Woods and was new to that part of town). By pairing John and Julie together in the cohort context around a topic both were genuinely passionate about, a natural space is created for organic relationship building where authentic mentorship and advocacy can take place between two leaders in the company.

After John and Julie were tapped to talk about the topic "Negotiating for What You Want," we prepped them. Participants identified questions to ask. As the Guest Mentors share their insights, the learning begins for everyone. For example, John may say, "The key is preparation. You need to have a good business case to succeed in negotiations." Then Julie might add that she needs more than a good business case, because as a woman leader, she has discovered she also has to be liked after the negotiation. John might ask, "What do you mean by that?" And the learning continues for him, too, but in a constructive, non-shaming way. In fact, by the time the experience is done, John has probably talked with a number of women in the organization and heard perspectives (and not just about negotiation, mind you) he simply didn't know before.

John learns from the women. Julie learns from John. And the women in the group cohort learn from both of them as the two share stories from the real world in Sheetz. This is what we refer to as vertical knowledge transfer, which is now layered in a thoughtful way on top of the consistent month-to-month, horizontal knowledge transfer between the peers. What makes the content truly relevant is that every dialogue takes place within the culture of Sheetz. It is all about "our company" and "our culture." It's about what actually works here and now: *When I'm negotiating for a raise here, what would you recommend I do?* Sheetz even took this approach to the next level by bringing in members of their board of directors as Guest Mentors—leaders above the C-Suite level and at the tops of their own Mountains—to engage with their front-line women.

When this type of full-circle knowledge transfer takes place, results get amplified exponentially. With horizontal knowledge transfer, people realize they're not alone, and yet everyone faces unique challenges depending on where they are on the Career and Life Growth Mountains. That's why vertical knowledge transfer is important. Peer coaching has an inherent limitation—we don't know what we don't know. As I mentioned earlier, in our PEER Framework, as knowledge is shared downward, perspective and feedback are shared upward. As it reaches the people at the top of the Mountain, they start looking differently at the needs of their employees. They start showing up differently and positively influence the people around them. It makes it possible over time for the entire company to change for the better.

With this cohort in particular, the 1:1 Career Interview tool had a significant impact. In this optional activity (remember Keri?), a cohort member chooses a leader, perhaps someone further up any Career or Life Growth Mountain, and asks to interview them. For example, if the cohort member's Outcome was to work on getting promoted inside Sheetz, they might choose to interview someone who could be a potential mentor or sponsor on their Internal Sheetz Career Growth Mountain. If they want to build their external network, they might choose a leader outside their company but inside their industry or community. If they want to focus on the Life Mountain, they might choose someone a little farther along in their area of interest, like interviewing people who are empty-nesters to learn best practices from them. We provide starter questions for when the interview takes place, but strongly encourage each person to choose questions based on their own desired EDGE outcome.

What this process does is give a pathway to build a relationship with somebody they normally wouldn't have access to. Then they come back to report on the Relevant Content they learned to the rest of the group, who in turn, should they choose to use it, now have an authentic leaping-off point with that executive to begin their own strategic network building. In that way, each cohort member grows their own knowledge base, connects with someone who may become a mentor or advocate, and shares that learning with others. Win. Win. Win.

As we moved forward with that initial Sheetz cohort, we added in the element of the **Practice Arena** and intentional developmental space for best practice sharing. The Mastermind is my vehicle of choice for this because it is so elegantly suited as a proven way to develop conversation, connection, and community.

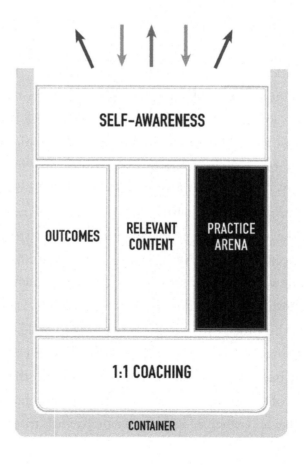

What I like most about the Mastermind is that it requires everyone to keep communication concise. The Masterminds meet every month in EDGE. (Even the Jumpstart, THRIVE, and Ignite Coaching Circles include a Mastermind element because best practice sharing is at the heart of the PEER Framework.) With a maximum of six minutes per person in groups of six, this structure creates the intentional space needed for some serious peer mentoring in less than forty minutes. With this Sheetz group of two dozen women meeting virtually, we found the best size for monthly Mastermind activities to be breakout rooms of six people, so introverts in the group didn't feel overwhelmed.

As always, we layer in choice. We don't want people to feel required to open up with our PEER Framework. We want to create a safe space and invite them to share. For example, we never go around in a circle, taking turns sharing. Instead, once someone volunteers and gives themselves permission to become vulnerable, the level of trust increases and more collective sharing takes place. People become inspired to share when they hear something in another person's story that resonates with or ignites them.

The Mastermind has three parts: Success, Challenge, and a Request for Support. We always start with Successes first, because there's a skill to be learned in being our own best advocate and standing in our own light. It's an effective way to practice building that muscle of sharing Successes. It doesn't have to be a raging Success, like if someone got a promotion. It can be that someone gave themselves permission to take a nap the previous weekend. Whatever Success is shared, I encourage coaches to create a way for other cohort members to celebrate it. A few ideas that have worked for me in the past include clapping, fingers snapping in front of the camera, whooping, and emojis/reactions when virtual, because there is tremendous value underpinning Success sharing. It's about the power of being recognized and people giving themselves permission to be seen. It's about celebrating the process of achievement in themselves and one another, instead of always just focusing on the next thing.

After sharing a Success, each person is invited to share a Challenge being faced right now. As with everything in the PEER Framework, we invite any of these responses to be personal as well as professional. One month a Challenge may be that someone needs to give difficult feedback to a boss. Next month they may need to give difficult feedback to a mother-in-law. PEER Group Coaching focuses on growing the person in order to to grow the leader. When we make progress up one Mountain in our life, we cannot help but see the ripple effects on the other Mountains in our range. (Never has this been more relevant than in our post-pandemic world, where our personal and professional lives often coexist in exactly the same space.)

After sharing a Challenge, members can make a "Request for Support" from the group. I encourage them to use those exact words. This language equips each person to better ask for help from others as they move forward, especially from other people who've gone through the PEER Group Coaching Framework.

Finally, after the Masterminds reconvene with the larger group, anyone can share a Request for Support with the larger group to access even more knowledge.

After more than twenty years of facilitating Masterminds, it is fascinating to me to see how people react to it differently. Sometimes these differences align across the gender spectrum. For example, with Sheetz, the women were all too happy to dive into Challenges each month, but often struggled to share Successes. I shared earlier why I think women struggle in this area, but this creates a real cost, both individually and corporately. If we do not know who has what skills and abilities in our network, how can we know who to call on when we encounter similar challenges? We are destined to recreate the wheel every time, instead of leveraging that shared knowledge and power.

Not surprisingly, the women in the Sheetz cohort also really struggled with asking for help. So we explored this theme in many **1:1 Coaching** sessions, through both Office Hours and Triad Coaching in the PEER Framework, and supported them to practice not only the skill of asking for help in their personal and professional lives, but also the art of giving themselves permission to receive help. In addition, we equipped them each to engage in 1:1 Coaching in Triads throughout the experience, a practice I'll describe in more detail later.

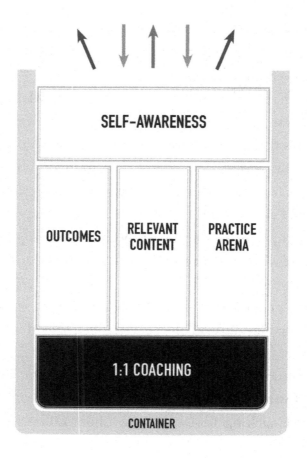

When the day came for their graduation from the program—in EDGE we call it their *Continuation*—the participants shared story after story of tremendous impact. Not surprisingly, given our content emphasis, the most impactful area to the cohort was coaching. That was certainly the case for Missy Forbes, Sheetz District Manager for Southern West Virginia. "I attended the 9-month EDGE experience. At Continuation, it was like I was being led through a dense Forest full of underbrush and trees, where cohort members are progressing on the path we can't see or understand, until the top of the mountain is reached and there is a clear view of the valley below."

For Strategic Planning Principal, Astral Cambruzzi, the experience shed light on the important role of coaching. "The most valuable takeaway for me was the coaching aspect of our training. I knew that throughout my career I have mentored others, given advice, and guided them, but I didn't know I was already coaching many people. I still use the Coaching Map Christy gave us to this day!"

These breakthrough experience stories are commonplace in these Continuation sessions. There is just no denying the growth that takes place from the group coaching experience, and the support received from this PEER Framework makes it possible for people to feel brave and vulnerable, sometimes for the first time.

Where does this courage, this vulnerability, come from? How do you help people feel safe enough to share their successes and challenges with others, willingly? It all starts with the Container.

IGNITE BEST PRACTICES

✓ Build the **Container,** which creates a safe place for participants to show up and share.

✓ Be intentional about **Self-Awareness.**

✓ Identify **Outcomes** for the group coaching experience. Always evaluate both the Outcomes desired by the company and the Outcomes desired by the people in the cohort. The PEER Group Coaching Framework is designed to do both.

✓ Ask the cohort members themselves what other **Relevant Content** they want to engage with in their experience, and enlist Guest Mentors, who provide enormous value, both to cohort members and to the Guest Mentors themselves.

✓ Provide a **Practice Arena,** an intentional developmental space for best practice sharing. The Mastermind is my vehicle of choice because it is elegantly suited as a proven way to develop conversation, connection, and community.

✓ Explore **1:1 Coaching** through Office Hours and Triad Coaching in the PEER Framework.

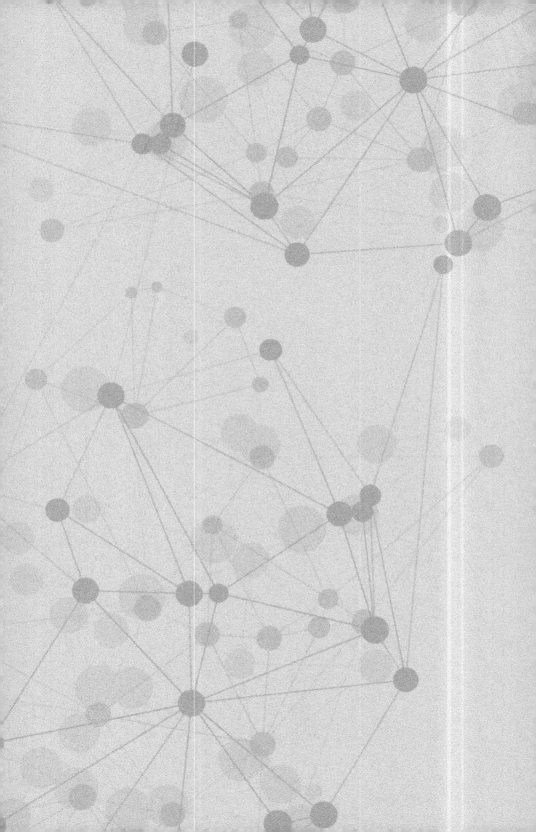

SECTION TWO:
THE FRAMEWORK

THE CONTAINER

*"Vulnerability is the birthplace of connection and
the path to the feeling of worthiness. If it doesn't feel
vulnerable, the sharing is probably not constructive."*

— D R .   B R E N É   B R O W N

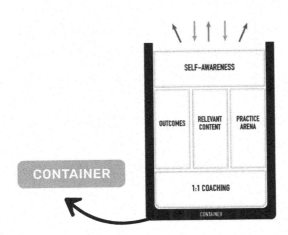

Have you ever gone to the beach and tried to scoop up sand with one hand? The tighter you try to hold it, the more the sand falls out of your hand. So it is with the group coaching environment. As coaches, we know we have to hold it *all* loosely. The tighter we try to control it, the more it eludes us. We create the Container. Then, we invite cohort members in.

When this is done well, amazing things can happen. We launched our first all-male cohort in 2014 (with the help of internal coach Michelle Buczkowski) with a coal and gas company. This was not with a diversity and inclusion focus, but simply because all of their high-potentials were, in fact, men. So, we already knew the PEER Framework worked in pretty incredible ways for men, when another one of our Fortune 50 clients came to us with a request. We had delivered four incredibly successful group coaching experiences for their women leaders. They wanted to know what we could offer in the spirit of helping men lead more inclusively? We launched our first Diversity, Equity, and Inclusion (DE&I) EDGE group coaching experience for men in 2017, a year before the #MeToo Movement. So by the time other organizations were ready to shift their thinking about the fact that #MenMatter in this conversation, we had already been witnessing powerful transformations with male leaders across multiple industries.

One group of men from DPR Construction launched their EDGE experience in San Diego in late 2017. These men came to call themselves "The Brotherhood." It was a cohort of men who truly changed my life. DPR Construction is a privately-held construction company, a self-performing general contractor focused on highly complex and technical projects. We had been delivering co-ed cohorts of mid-career leaders across the US with them for a few years. Always trying to innovate when it comes to culture, the leader of DPR's Learning and Development team, Cari Williams, decided to challenge the status quo. If they truly wanted to shift the mindsets of male leaders, perhaps we could turbo charge the shift by separating group coaching cohorts across the gender spectrum.

I loved the idea, and here's why: What I had seen in the ten years prior, when working with cohorts in both Early Career Field and the Mid-Career Woods, was in co-ed peer groups, women often lost their voices. We could argue whether they "gave it up" in deference to the men (who were the vast majority in the groups) or if the men simply "overpowered" the few women's voices in the room. But the effect was real. I also watched men, in the presence of women, side step vulnerability. They told me they simply didn't feel safe as a man to be vulnerable in front of female colleagues. The company decided to pilot two gender-specific cohorts, one each with those self-identifying as women or men.

From day one, the men's group jumped ALL IN. As the lone woman in the room, and their group coach for the next nine months, I knew I couldn't force engagement in any way. I had to keep my palm open, as it were, to support them as they, themselves, created a Container in which they could feel it was safe to choose to be vulnerable. I watched these men give themselves permission to peel back the layers, beginning with their professional selves, to their insecurities on the job site as people managers overwhelmed with the busyness of work, to their personal lives and tremendous fears of inadequacy as husbands, partners, fathers, siblings, and sons.

They chose to step into that Brotherhood environment in those first two days of our Launch. Then, they showed up powerfully for one another every month thereafter. When the

DPR Management Committee members joined us as Guest Mentors at the Midpoint session of the experience, one of the guys described this Brotherhood as being similar to what he had felt at only one other time in life—in the military. He felt as if they were truly back-to-back, each trusting the next guy with his life, as together they faced common enemies.

One of the best bits of feedback I've ever received came from a man in that group at their Continuation: "When I started this nine months ago, I thought it was going to be a typical leadership development training. It was never that, not once. It was one of the most defining experiences of my life, and I want you to know that I am leaving here a better husband and father because of this. Thank you." That is what can happen when we first create the Container in which cohort members feel psychologically safe to be truly vulnerable and show up as a whole person in a professional setting.

A SAFE SPACE TO SHARE

It's difficult to overestimate the importance of vulnerability when it comes to achieving higher levels of personal and professional success. It all starts with the courage to take a risk and share your story. When what is shared gets validated, it promotes an environment of support and encouragement. On the other hand, vulnerability without validation and empathy can cause harm. This is why the Container is so critical. The result is a place where it is safe

"There is no innovation without vulnerability."

to talk openly and honestly—that's when human potential can really take off.

Everything depends on the level of vulnerability people are willing to show. Just like in my opening story of this book, when people give themselves permission to be vulnerable, they challenge the stories they are writing and step into purposeful Self-Awareness and growth. They are willing to explore negative self-talk and the push back on the inner critic that keeps them feeling small and stuck. They allow themselves to risk judgment in sharing messy insights in the group experience and being open to others' perspectives on it. There is no innovation without vulnerability. We cannot iterate and choose new actions until we step forward—as a beginning—and make new choices. It is this vulnerability that fosters the intimacy needed to build dynamic, connecting, and collaborative relationships.

> "The truth is, we think we most fear the judgement of others, but in reality, no one judges us more harshly than we judge ourselves."

But how do we overcome the barriers that keep a group of people from opening up? Vulnerability often feels scary, revealing, and exposing. Talking about yourself can feel fraught with peril, especially with (gulp) work colleagues—and it can be, if you don't know what you're doing. But the truth is, without vulnerability, human potential is limited.

Group coaching can fail—quite spectacularly—if we do not purposefully create a safe space for success, because people must feel empowered to take what they perceive to be a huge risk—the risk of being judged. When they see a cohort member step into the light and share something important to them, they cannot help but feel touched by the common humanity. *Me too*, our hearts say. *Me too*. And the truth is, we think we most fear the judgment of others, but in reality, *no one* judges us more harshly than we judge ourselves. As adults, we have become so used to hearing that harsh judgement in our own heads and hearts, we just assume others will do the same or worse. So we "armor up," as Dr. Brené Brown calls it. But as I said earlier, vulnerability begets vulnerability.

When I met Christy, I knew the PEER experience was different. We piloted a cohort of forty leaders with Christy focusing on four leadership competencies, coaching in all areas utilizing multiple techniques. She did a very nice job incorporating vulnerability into the group coaching experience and forming personal connections with team members through her enthusiasm and own vulnerability. Her goal was to build an all-inclusive, down-to-earth approach to connect people with people.

—Todd W. Faulk,
Vice President of Human Resources, Duquesne Light Company

One by one, each person is inspired by the one who spoke before them, each becoming more and more comfortable sharing their personal and professional selves. They can truly let themselves be seen by contributing in a way that is transparent with one another and without judgment.

SHOUT OUTS

When closing each PEER Group Coaching session, it's important to give the cohort members' voices center stage every single time to help maintain the Container. At the end of every session, I encourage what I call "Shout Outs," where people give recognition to others who have made an impact on them. Even if it's just a 2-hour experience, I promise that someone made a positive impact to most everyone. By sharing a little gratitude, it lets them know the depth of their impact.

These Shout Outs are dedicated times where cohort members can give one another a special mention, but it's up to each person how they do it. Shout Outs are beautiful gestures that can reinforce success or progress toward achieving Outcomes. They are also a great way for someone else to acknowledge the positive impact a peer has had on them, whomever it may be in the group.

A word of caution: if the coach is the one receiving most of the Shout Outs, *something is wrong*. At least 95% of these Shout Outs should be directed toward fellow peers who have shared knowledge and insights or offered support.

At the end of the entire group coaching experience, it is also important to the Container to plan a closing ritual at Graduation that takes the concept of Shout Outs to a deeper and more meaningful level. This allows everyone to reflect back on their journey and on what they got out of it. This time also allows people to express gratitude, practice vulnerability, and say what's on their hearts.

THE CONTINUATION

Just like in 1:1 Coaching, our goal as coaches is to create an environment of gentle irreverence—where people can open up while simultaneously allowing themselves to

"Growth doesn't happen when we stay in our comfort zone."

be challenged. If we're good coaches, we'll consistently make them a little uncomfortable, because that is how all of us grow. In the PEER Framework, the coach masterfully co-creates a space with their group by first setting the stage and modeling vulnerability. We must be willing to bring our whole self to meet them there as a peer and to authentically practice vulnerability ourselves. We cannot merely tell everyone else in the group that it is important, like a trainer clicking on a PowerPoint slide deck. Because growth simply doesn't happen when we stay in our comfort zone.

Consistency matters throughout the experience when building and maintaining the Container. And so does how you close out the PEER experience as a whole. In the EDGE experience, it all comes together in the final graduation session which we call the Continuation, because it is anything but the end. It is merely the beginning of the next phase of living out what cohort members have learned. Executive leaders are invited well in advance. It is such a special event for the members that some cohorts invite partners and spouses to hear them share these transformation stories, always in a heartfelt and vulnerable way.

This one-hour Continuation presentation has three parts: Introduction, Stories of Impact, and Pay It Forward. The Introduction lasts about ten minutes, and allows officers and attendees to get to know cohort members' names and faces. Many cohorts choose to create a video featuring each participant, and sometimes layer in music that serves as an anthem for the group. During the Stories of Impact, cohort members spend around thirty minutes delivering TED talk-style presentations, sharing personal stories that demonstrate how their lives were changed as a result of their 9-month group coaching experience.

At the end of the presentation, the group typically presents how they will Pay It Forward. Beginning at the Midpoint of the entire experience, the cohort together invests time to decide how they will give back to others in light of what they have learned. In many ways, the Pay It Forward component is like the return on investment (ROI) for the company. It channels the parts and pieces of the PEER experience that changed everyone's lives to create a cascading effect throughout the rest of the organization. It may be an intentional effort to teach direct reports how to coach and use the Coaching Map. It may be involvement in the community. It can be anything the cohort decides represents them as their leadership brand.

All this together explains why so many organizational leaders love the Continuation—they get to hear stories of growth and directly discover the power of the PEER experience. The responses are not filtered through talent management or HR. Corporate leaders actually see people tear up and say, *This experience has changed my life, transformed my marriage, or elevated my leadership. Now I want to pay it forward.* In other words, it is every executive's dream.

SETTING THE STAGE FOR SUCCESS

The PEER Framework's seven best practices for creating the Container can be layered into any leadership development content or group coaching program. Although the context is different for each group, the Container remains exactly the same. You carry out the same steps every single time, because people are people. They're going to show up and want to contribute to each other, I promise you. When they contribute, it increases confidence. When confidence increases, it allows people to be more vulnerable. Thus, the Container is about creating the space of connection through vulnerability, intimacy, and a community of relationships.

We must not only create the Container, but also purposely maintain it throughout the group coaching experience, whether that is for two hours, two days, or nine months. Maintaining the Container means modeling vulnerability throughout the entire time. As a coach, you can't simply be vulnerable in the Launch and think the work is done. You have to continue to circle back around to it and let the people accompany you on your own journey and individual Outcomes, just as you do the same for them. Remember, unlike mentoring or advocating, coaching is an equal power relationship. Group coaching is no different. We are there to companion them and give them permission, in turn, to companion us. Even as the group coach, I am also a peer, so I identify an Outcome I want for myself every time I lead a group through this PEER process. It's never the same because I'm different each month and year. As a result, every cohort and every context is unique.

It was reassuring to be surrounded by these successful women who I could tell were going places, but that were also kicking ass in all aspects of their lives. I learned a lot about balance from these women, including the fact that it's ok to say "No." I got comfortable with the uncomfortable. From meeting with partners I'd never met before to presenting to clients that included some of the top executives in the city, I learned to settle into my space and feel a confidence greater than ever before. I am continuing to get comfortable being uncomfortable, specifically with coaching my team. I'm not afraid to have hard conversations now because I know that it will only help that person and myself moving forward.

—Carley Taslov,
Senior Manager Risk Advisory Services, Schneider Downs

Before we unpack the seven best practices for creating the Container, it is vital to note two things. First, the majority of what I describe next will occur in the Launch session of the 9-month EDGE experience. For the Jumpstart, THRIVE, or Ignite Coaching Circles, you may apply some of these, but at a much higher level. Second, the concept of *choice* is absolutely critical to success in Container building. In every activity, engagement happens only through choice. No one should be forced to do, say, or share anything they don't want to.

When participants move into small breakout groups, I remind them there is just as much value in sharing a story as there is in holding the space for someone else to share. Just like the analogy of the open hands holding the sand, the Container is held by those who aren't speaking for those who choose to speak. Participants are always going to be stepping in and out of those two roles.

So often in adult learning, we praise the extroverts, the people who speak up as if that is the "right way" to do it. But putting pressure on people causes them not to share the real stuff. Giving them the choice honors all learning styles, including the more introverted styles who maybe aren't comfortable sharing right away. For example, one guy in an all-male cohort of coal miners under the age of thirty didn't speak in the large group setting until the next-to-last month we were together. But when he did, his powerful voice impacted us *all*. He had been listening closely and engaging at his own pace. He held the Container.

That is why it is really important throughout the experience to give people the choice. The concept of choice is absolutely critical to creating, maintaining, and thoughtfully closing the

Container. Always. Even in the closing ritual, we never call on anybody. Ever.

When the eight best practices are done well, the result is connection, contribution, and community within the cohort.

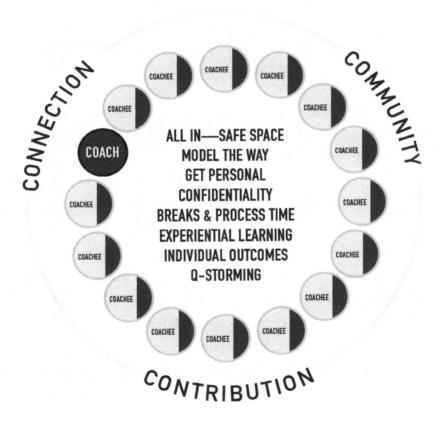

ALL IN—SAFE SPACE
MODEL THE WAY
GET PERSONAL
CONFIDENTIALITY
BREAKS & PROCESS TIME
EXPERIENTIAL LEARNING
INDIVIDUAL OUTCOMES
Q-STORMING

* Shading in the coachee denotes the role of coach played by all cohort members.

EIGHT CONTAINER-CREATING PRACTICES

1. Choosing to be "ALL IN"

Offering your cohort participants choice needs to have some definition, otherwise people don't know what is possible and what that can look like for them. The structure comes to life with our PEER Vulnerability Levels. It gives people three choices as to their level of engagement:

- **Head:** The professional, cerebral, surface level. Answers here often sound like how you would respond in a typical, corporate training class, where the instructor calls on you and you give them the "right" answer. (It's the answer that reinforces your brand in the room, and, while it is often true, it isn't usually the *whole* truth.)

- **Heart:** The emotional level. You will know you are in this place because you will begin to feel it physiologically in your body when you respond. Answers could include things such as talking about my grandmother's passing last October, and I can feel the words getting caught in my throat. Or, I may share about my colleague, who I think is trying to sabotage a team project, and I can feel my jaw start to clench as I speak.

- **Belly:** The deep level of your truth. I don't know about you, but I can get myself into trouble by always listening to my Head. (I can talk myself in or out of almost anything.) Sometimes, I get in trouble when my emotions overcome me at the Heart level. But *very rarely* do I get into trouble when I listen to my Belly. Your Belly (or Gut) is where your intuition and deep wisdom lives.

THE VULNERABILITY CHOICE

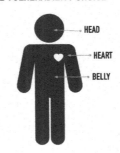

Each level reveals more about me as an individual as I give myself permission to become a little bit more vulnerable. As you begin to build the Container, the powerful invitation at hand is to be intentional with your cohort about the choice they have to engage from their Head, Heart, or Belly in each and every conversation.

When you provide a vulnerability paradigm like this right up front, as I do in every single group coaching experience, no matter the length of time, you invite people to recognize exactly *how much choice* they really do have. As you lead the experience, I encourage you to offer true examples for each of these levels as you explain them. Leverage the teaching moment as a moment to model vulnerability as well. How much you choose to reveal in your responses about yourself is completely up to you. What I can promise you is that if you dip your toe into vulnerability, so will they. If you wade in up to your knees, they will follow. And if you jump ALL IN, you better believe you will hear several splashes alongside you in pretty short order.

As an introvert myself, the PEER Group Coaching experience was built with introverted leaders in mind. As such, we never call on anyone. When I have a question, I will float it into the center of the room and let the cohort choose to respond. You will find that more of the group will engage in that way with Heart and Belly, and conversations will be so much richer for it.

In that same vein, if someone answers a question, and I have a probing follow-up question as the group coach, I will not ask it of them without knowing they are open to it. For example, suppose I were to ask someone to share about what they are taking away from the pre-work activity. When I hear Dawnita's response, I am curious and want to know more. Instead of asking, "Dawnita, can you give me an example?" I say, "Dawnita brings up a great point. Who would be willing to share an example of how that shows up for you?" Then Dawnita can jump in if she chooses, and, if not, that is okay, too. Either way, I receive a deeper response to my question (which is what I want in the first place).

I invite all who are at the Belly level for any conversation to write "ALL IN" next to their screen name for virtual sessions. (For in-person sessions, we have ready made stickers they can wear, like a name tag.) This tells everyone that the person is willing to engage at a deeper level of conversation and gives us all permission to ask additional questions or offer coaching in-the-moment.

2. Model the Way

An opening story builds intimacy. A relatable story deepens vulnerability and is vital to creating the Container. But to become a coach, as we all know, you have to get in touch with your shadow side. You've got to learn to sit in your own dark places and make sense of them. As a coach, ready to implement group coaching into your practice or company, I invite you to ask yourself some key questions:

- ► How comfortable am I with being vulnerable?
- ► What work could I do on vulnerability as I step into this?
- ► Where do I struggle? Why?
- ► What is hard for me right now? How?

In all my PEER Group Coaching Launches, I open with a story about a challenge at work first (because my audience is all corporate types), and transition shortly thereafter at another point in time with a current challenge in my marriage—both super relatable. Even if somebody is not married, everyone is in an intimate relationship, has been in one, or likely wants to be in one. So it's important to find a relatable and vulnerable story. But it *has* to be authentic.

It's really important when you model vulnerability to bring your own real challenges, not use a story from three years ago or make things up. If you're in a really great place in your marriage, don't use marriage challenges as an example because it will come across as inauthentic. The lack of authenticity can make participants not trust you from that point forward. Pick a story that is relatable, but also equally relevant to you right now.

Don't just tell the story and move on. Circle back to it throughout the agenda—when you all define your individual Outcomes, for example—and again as an update in later sessions. When you weave your story back in, you invite them to share in it and to support your work on it, even as you model what you want them to do. A group coach is a peer, after all. Just like each and every member of the cohort, we are imperfect. And, as we embrace our imperfections, we invite them to do the same.

> My PEER experience helped me immediately rethink and reprioritize my life, both at work and at home. This helped decrease stress and anxiety levels, reduced "mom guilt," and increased my confidence and productivity, which ultimately led to my ability to deliver more value to my company and be a happier wife and mom.
>
> **—Katie Nelson,**
> *Business Analytics Manager, PNC Bank*

In every session, I open with their voices and close with their voices—remember, even though we are responsible for helping to shape it, it is *their* Container. So although the best practice is to open with a personal story, you'll want to quickly get them into small breakout groups sharing their stories. And because you modeled what sharing your story looks like, now it's easier for them to share their stories. After their voices are heard, bring the small groups back into large group conversations. Take the small Container trust-building and bleed it back into the larger Container. Then trust can start to flow and ignite all the corners of the group.

As group coaches, unlike typical corporate training classes, I recommend that the stories you share be personal 75% of the time. Only 25% of the sharing you do should be relevant to work. If you're a coach working with entrepreneurs, that 25% would then be related to entrepreneurship. If you're working with parents, the 25% focus would be related to parenting or whatever the domain of your group. The personal piece of it is really important because the personal is the most universal.

I do this because examples I share about work may or may not resonate with everybody, but the personal ones consistently do. Everybody has a parent or grandparent. People have siblings, cousins, and neighbors. Lots of people have intimate relationships—children, nieces, nephews, or young people in their lives who they want to impact. Choose stories that are truly authentic to you but relatable to everyone.

A few cautionary thoughts on this, however. First, don't open a door you can't close. Depending on how much time you have with people, it is very important to self-monitor the level of intimacy you create. For example, I share different levels of my story with different groups. If I'm on a 6- or 9-month journey with them, I'll share much more than I do with a 2-hour or

2-day experience. Even after doing this work for more than twenty years, I cannot open up the space for people to have really dramatic breakthroughs in two hours or two days. I simply won't be there to coach them through it on day three. But if we're together for nine months, and they're getting some 1:1 Coaching from me and from their peers throughout the journey, these layers of support can be really important and allow us to go deeper into personal growth. After all, this is why so many of us got into the field of coaching in the first place—to ignite and fan the flames of transformation.

Second, don't go overboard and share what you're going through right now without having processed it first. When you do, your participants become your caretakers, trying to console you because you can't get through your own story without crying. Sure, you're being vulnerable, but now the experience has become all about you. Your story has to be real, but it also has to be something that you have processed in a healthy way.

A third lesson I've learned (which I hate, but it's true) is to use caution when sharing parts of your story that other people may have biases against, at least until they get to know you as a person first. For example, if you are in the LGBTQ+ community, and your cohort is made up of mid-level managers in a high-potential program, I suggest not revealing that until you have built more trust and vulnerability in the relationship. After all, sexuality is a very small part of who people are within this context. Now, if your cohort is the LGBTQ+ EBRG inside a corporation, well then, jump right in, my friends! I have seen some members of cohorts shut out coaches right from the outset because they shared something about themselves that went against typical systemic biases. They decided right there in the first hour that they could not relate. I invite you to be authentic and also to gauge your audience (and what research shows us as common unconscious bias). Think: both/and not either/or. To be clear, I am not suggesting that you not be your true self. Just be thoughtful and choose the timing of what you share and when.

3. Get Personal

The Container is always about the cohort members. It can never be about you. So you want to model that for them by not putting the spotlight on yourself. You're igniting and empowering the group to reflect their own light back to one another. The spotlight is not, and should not be, on you, but you do need to model getting personal first.

> "If we truly want to influence people, expand mindsets, and bust bias, then we have to remind them of how connected we are—how much we are alike—before they see how we are different."

Over the years, what I have learned to do as I am preparing for my sessions is to check in with myself and ask, *Where am I struggling right now in my personal life? What could be better? What's hard for me right now? What's keeping me up at night?* I find something authentic, but still not so raw and unprocessed where I'm crying in front of the group. I've seen that happen, and it's not good.

Once you're about 25% into the Launch session by sharing your story initially, then you'll want to bring in your whole self, but only after you build trust and credibility with your cohort members for the whole person you are. Once again, it's important to recognize that society is imperfect, and people have biases and don't always agree. For example, for most cohort audiences, I usually do not lead in my opening story with the fact that I have a transgender son, but you better believe that by the end of day one (even in the 2-day Jumpstart) I've mentioned it, because it is part of who I am. If we truly want to influence people, expand mindsets, and bust bias, then we have to remind them of how connected we are—how much we are alike—before they see how we are different.

We coaches are people too, and it has been my experience that we judge ourselves far more harshly than others judge us. You may recognize a few frequently used judgmental phrases like, *I need to..., I have to..., I should....* All of us have used them and heard others do the same. Experienced group coaches see the judgment of others as fear that sits on the surface. The deeper fear comes from the judgment we have of ourselves and the voice of our own inner critic.

How do you create a space where people can gently call one another out when we start judging ourselves? You go first, then you acknowledge any personal stories that are shared without digging too far into them. Remember, we are not therapists. We are coaches. Therapy is turning the person around, looking back at their life and saying, "Let's look at what happened and how it is showing up in your life now." Coaching focuses on where the person is now and where they want to go from here.

4. Code of Confidentiality

By the time you are about 50% through your Launch time (Visit Edge LeadershipSolutions.com for a sample agenda), you've invested in the group and created some type of confidentiality where you develop trust. You will want to make sure confidentiality is already created before you go to the next level of intimacy. Then, you are asking people to really open up and unveil their fears and dreams. They're only going to do that when they feel like what they say will be kept sacred.

Once you've created that confidential space, your job as the coach is a lot like widening a tunnel you have built. You can only widen it if you have the right equipment in place. (I learned this during my time down in the coal mines, where the tunnels were often so large you could fit two cars side-by-side—one coming, and one going!) And the reality is we can only dig so much ourselves. Confidentiality empowers you to engage in more robust, transformative, development activities because now you have more room in the tunnel.

Build relationships. Practice vulnerability. Connect people. Then, talk about trust, and what would happen if they had greater trust at work (or in whatever domain you are offering your group coaching). Invite them into a conversation about what could happen if they had more trust at home or in their personal relationships. There would be less stress. They would sleep better at night. And on and on. This is all part of having the participants co-create a code of confidentiality. Remember, just like in 1:1 Coaching, folks live along a spectrum of trust. Some people arrive ready to trust until they are proven wrong. Others arrive with the mindset that you've got to earn their trust. Everyone is different and has different needs. This will become apparent quickly when you have a group of two dozen leaders chiming in.

As a coach, it is critical to really be in the moment with your people as you establish this code of confidentiality. Sometimes this conversation can last twenty minutes. Sometimes it can last an hour or longer, depending on the particular group's needs. Stay purposefully beside them, and adjust your expectations as required.

One important thing to know: avoid turning their words into your words. I recommend that you capture their code on a virtual whiteboard to save to the group's Teams or Sharepoint site for easy reference later. As you listen, write down the exact same language, terms, and expressions they use. When you convert their words into what *you* think they should be, you can sometimes lose the fledgling trust you spent the last few hours building because it can be seen as judgment. You are essentially saying their description wasn't good enough. It needed translating. When you do that, you unintentionally discount what they're saying.

As a coach, you may have or develop other vehicles to create this code of confidentiality and that is perfectly fine. Use what works for you. It is similar to building a house; the foundational and structural elements need to be in place for any house, but the trim and decor can differ. Every house needs walls, for example, but every house can feature different siding or or window styles within those walls. Your details may be unique to you, but the core elements need to be present for the group coaching house to stand.

5. Include Breaks and Process Time

When you're done with confidentiality, but before you get to a deepening activity (as described in the next best practice), it's really important to take a break immediately after you complete the code of confidentiality. Take time to shake it off. Play some upbeat music on a playlist you invite the cohort to co-create with you—I like to call them "anthems". Just like hearing "your song" in the car puts you instantly in a good mood and might make you want to roll the windows down and turn up the volume, creating a customized playlist for each cohort can really elevate the mood in the room. So when they're on breaks, or whenever the activities are taking place, the best practice is to play their customized songs in the background.

Taking breaks is especially important during a potentially polarizing activity like when people are talking about confidentiality. You don't want them carrying any of that intense energy into the next activity because people naturally self-censor. Without time to process and decompress, walls can go up and inhibitions grow. Always give participants intentional breaks and processing time.

Just like you can become burned out when you don't take breaks during a workday, it's important to take breaks in the group coaching day to maintain the Container. For every ninety minutes of activity, provide a fifteen-minute break to process and decompress. This is especially important for virtual cohorts who need a break away from their screens.

It's important to encourage participants to take care of themselves, to get a fresh cup of coffee, check in on a family member, or just relax. I often take this a step farther in virtual groups by having individual reflection time inside an activity where participants leave the screens and go sit somewhere else. They can take a picture of the prompt on the screen, grab a journal and reflect, then come back and share with the group.

6. Experiential Learning (EXL)

The Container is co-created by the participants, so you can't just think you can do it all as a large group when some participants are more introverted folks who likely will not be as comfortable. The more experiential learning (EXL) opportunities you can build in with small breakout groups or partnering activities, the more flexible the Container will ultimately become. This flexibility amplifies the power of the Container.

Once confidentiality is agreed upon, I recommend having some kind of activity in the Launch of our longer group coaching experiences that empowers them to reflect both individually and together. Have them look back, ideally through a personal lens, at what has influenced them to become the individual, the leader, they are today. Because in truth, we can't design the second half of the group coaching experience until we know where we are. And we can't fully know where we are until we look around and evaluate where we came from.

Each person will gain value from evaluating the stories that they carry (think of me in my opening tale, or Michelle in hers) and ask, *What has influenced who I've become? What am I lugging around that is maybe not serving me?* I call it clearing the mental clutter or creating white space. We can label it differently, but it's all about people taking stock of where they are, and it is vital to the coaching process that we do it as a group.

No matter where I want to go, I can only chart my path if I know the starting point. Help people find their starting point. This is no different than what we do in our intake in 1:1 Coaching, only now we want to create the space not only for reflection, but also for people to step into the PEER vulnerability levels and choose to share their stories with one another. Each story amplifies the circle of the Container.

"Even a positive judgment is still a judgment."

I like to use an activity called "I Am From History." I don't claim to have created this widely used activity—it is one that I've experienced personally and found it to be powerful in my own development. It starts off with the lead-in phrase "I am from…" and then participants fill in the blanks. No additional rules. They just complete the phrase however they see fit, in whatever way they wish.

Often when somebody shares their "I Am From History", it is incredibly powerful. People might cry, and as a coach, you may get choked up yourself. But the most valuable best practice I can offer you is to *not* say, "That was beautiful" or "Wow. That was so powerful," because even a positive judgment is still a judgment. When other participants hear this judgment, they naturally begin to compare and critique their own stories (or worse, they decide to not share at all). Instead of giving praise, I invite you to simply say, "Thank you." Every time someone shares, no matter what they share, just say, "Thank you." That's it. By doing that, you model the way and hold that space in the Container for them to share.

One example of the transforming possibility of this activity is that of Stephanie Rideau. She had attended one of our 2-day Jumpstart group coaching experiences in 2018 where a personal transformation process began. As she describes it:

> Two powerful things happened. I realized I was not alone with the "inner critic" that liked to rise up and share a few words with me. I was shocked at the number of women who experienced this same thing.

> The second thing is, I gave myself permission not to be perfect, but to learn. I gave myself permission to rest, and not be consumed with "getting it right" all the time. I began to manifest courage, confidence, and peace. Even though I looked the same on the outside, my internal self-talk had improved.

> My mindset was changing from critical perfectionist to growth, finding joy and learning in the journey. During this time, I practiced new ways to better manage my inner critic. My confidence began to bloom. Ironically, when I gave myself permission to not get it right, I started getting it right.

As an African American woman, Stephanie would sometimes measure herself with a different yardstick and felt she had to be perfect in everything and not make any mistakes. She was reared to think she couldn't just be good; she had to be twice as good.

As a result, she felt a lot of pressure and a heavy load to carry. But she knew there was more to her than gender or skin color. She was smart, resilient, and resourceful.

As she continued to apply what she had gained from the Jumpstart experience, Stephanie applied for a promotion and started a new role. She soon discovered that the higher level provided plenty of new opportunities to doubt herself and her skills, so she leaned into the peer group she had formed for accountability and support. After a year, Stephanie Rideau's Outcomes at work began to exponentially improve. She felt good, innovating and crushing her goals. She was driving results, developing people, and creating a great company culture for her team. Stephanie was thinking differently and had the confidence to try something new. As a result, she launched several initiatives that were shared and adopted at a division level inside her national organization.

Within the following year, Stephanie received a call about a new opportunity based on her leadership and performance. This new opportunity led to her securing a new promotion, which Stephanie started in the fall of 2020—moving across the country mid-pandemic.

The inner critic that had been previously tamed in Stephanie began to rise up again. She found herself in new territory with so much she didn't know. Stephanie started our 9-month EDGE experience shortly afterwards. As she engaged in the "I Am From History" activity, her inner critic reared up again, reminding her of what she didn't have and what she didn't know.

But when she read her "I Am" statement, something happened within. As she finished reading it, she realized her past didn't define her. It is a part of her, but not all of her. It is her collective experience that impacts her. She realized that she is a victor, not a victim.

At that point, Stephanie started rewriting her "I Am" statement. As she did, she realized how much she had overcome to get there. During the EDGE Launch, cohort members each create a folder that represents what they want to accomplish over the course of their nine months together. For Stephanie, hers included growth, courage, light, and confidence.

As a result of this work, Stephanie began to make friends with her inner critic for the first time and stopped trying simply to "manage" her. She gave herself permission to say that she doesn't represent all Black women. In fact, she doesn't even represent all women. She simply represents herself. She began focusing on adding value where she was and felt the heaviness slip off her shoulders.

The work that had begun in 2018 internally truly started to manifest itself externally as the seeds of the 2-day Jumpstart grew in the intentional fertile soil of EDGE group coaching.

7. Q-Storming

Teaching cohort members how to coach so they can peer coach one another is foundational to the Container and the entire group coaching experience. However, as any good coach knows, before you teach someone how to coach, you first have to teach them how to listen and create the space to start building the foundational skill of asking questions (versus offering solutions) and active listening. The best practice I offer you is to avoid teaching heavy-duty coaching material right away. What you do want is for them to be vulnerable and to practice sitting in the discomfort of wanting to tell somebody what to do, but *not* telling that somebody what to do.

Q-storming is a fabulous experiential learning activity to use in the Launch designed to help them do both. (Once again, this activity is not original to me. Several different versions exist.) First, somebody volunteers to be a "Brave Soul." A couple of volunteers act as scribes while the Brave Soul practices vulnerability and shares a challenge they are facing. (Don't worry, if you've done even a decent job of establishing the Container to this point, you'll have several people volunteer.) That said, try to listen to your intuition and pick a person you think will share a personal story, not a professional story. This activity builds more intimacy and relationships for the container when somebody shares a relatable, personal story.

Once our Brave Soul shares a story around a current challenge, the group asks Clarifying Questions first, facilitated by the group coach. This helps participants better understand the story. The group asks these questions so they can understand the challenge at hand. The Brave Soul responds to their questions with the details as requested. Then, at some point, the coach transitions the second part of the process to move into more Reflective Questions (foundational coaching questions). Reflective Questions are generated by the group in the moment with some guidance from the coach and are always asked in the first person to protect the Brave Soul from feeling judged. Examples could include, *What do I most want out of this and why? What is keeping me up at night? What haven't I tried yet? Where and how am I holding back?* Unlike with the Clarifying Questions, these questions are *not answered* by the Brave Soul. (Now that person gets to simply sit and listen to these questions as the scribes capture them in the question asker's own words.)

For example, if someone shares a story about communication issues with a partner at home, the group coach will encourage the group to ask specific, relevant questions that the Brave Soul can reflect on later to decide what to do next and how. These questions will get that person thinking about the issue from a different perspective and create the space for a mindset shift.

Think about Clarifying Questions like a giant ear, because they bring value only to the listeners (to help us better understand the challenge at hand: the context, background, and emotions). Reflective Questions then act like a giant mirror that allows the Brave Soul to see themselves and reflect on their mindset—their story. The value of the Reflective Questions is solely for them and their development.

It is important that the questions are asked in the first person. For example, "What would I do if I had no fear?" Once again, these questions are *not* answered aloud by our Brave Soul, but exist solely to help shift their own mindset around the challenge. Nevertheless, I repeatedly hear from cohort members that the questions bring value to all equally.

8. Set Individual Outcomes

The process of leveraging EXL activities to support cohort members as they reflect is all about forming connections. It is about seeing the sparks of light reflected in one another's past and current stories and about recognizing that we have far more in common than we know. In contrast, looking forward is all about achieving your individual Outcomes. It's their answer to this question: *What do you want to get out of this?*

Now participants are ready to ask themselves that question. It's always a good idea to give participants the choice (always a choice!) to discover their individual Outcomes individually or in groups. Think of this as Part 2 of the group coaching intake experience. For the Launch session, I simply ask them to raise a hand virtually if they want to be placed into groups to discuss possibilities together. Otherwise, we'll all meet back in forty-five minutes after they each work on a right-brained creative activity that supports them as they each determine their own individual Outcomes.

Then I put people together who chose to be in groups, play some upbeat music, and let them chit-chat. They coach one another to wrap words around what they want to accomplish in the 9-month peer group journey (and how they will know when they get there!).

These eight best practices will help you create a Container you can maintain and build on throughout the PEER Group Coaching experience. Obviously, the entire process pivots on Self-Awareness, the next essential piece of the process.

IGNITE BEST PRACTICES

✓ Hold the Container loosely. The more you try to control it, the more it will elude you.

✓ Vulnerability is extremely important when it comes to achieving higher levels of personal and professional success. When sharing is met with empathy, it promotes an environment of support, encouragement, and innovation.

✓ Never call on anyone to contribute. Ever. Holding silence is one of the most powerful things in the group. Someone always speaks up. Always.

✓ Most people fear the judgment of others, but in reality, no one judges us more harshly than we judge ourselves.

✓ Even a positive judgment is still a judgment. After someone shares, resist the urge to praise. Simply say, "Thank you."

✓ The Container is about creating the space of connection through vulnerability, intimacy, and a community of relationships. It must be maintained by modeling vulnerability as the group coach throughout the entire experience.

To recap: the 8 Best Practices to Build the Container are as follows:

✓ **Encourage the Group to Be All-In:** Be intentional with your cohort about the choice they have to engage from their Head, Heart, or Belly.

- **The Head:** The cerebral, superficial (often "professional") level.
- **The Heart:** The emotional level.
- **The Belly:** The deep level of your truth.

✓ **Model the Way:** Offer an opening story to build intimacy and model vulnerability.

✓ **Get Personal:** Once you're about 25% into the Launch session by sharing your story, bring in your whole self.

✓ **Code of Confidentiality:** Around 50% through your Launch time, engage the participants to co-create their code of confidentiality.

✓ **Include Intentional Breaks and Process Time:** Take purposeful breaks and offer reflection time away from their screens.

✓ **Experiential Learning (EXL):** Layer activities throughout the Launch to empower participants to reflect on their learnings both in small breakouts and larger debriefs.

✓ **Q-Storming:** A "Brave Soul" shares a challenge they are facing, then the group asks questions facilitated by the group coach to seed coaching skills building.

✓ **Set Individual Outcomes:** Looking forward is all about each cohort member wrapping language around achieving their individual Outcomes. *Invite them to identify what they want to get out of this.*

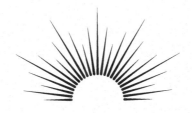

THOUGHT SPARKS

1. *What resonated most with you in this chapter? Why?*

2. *What questions do you still have?*

3. *How do you go about establishing the Container (either in group processing or in 1:1 Coaching) now? What works well? What could be better?*

4. To what extent are you "ALL IN" when coaching? Do you find yourself existing mostly in your Head, Heart, or Belly right now at work? At home?

5. What is the cost of not building the Container well? What is one area in which you want to be more intentional about deploying?

SELF-AWARENESS

"Man is not what he thinks he is, he is what he hides."

—ANDRÉ MALRAUX

As a coach, you probably think you've heard everything there is to know about Self-Awareness, right? But before you skip this chapter, let's back up a minute and make sure we're talking about the same thing. What do we actually mean by *Self-Awareness*? In my experience, it's far more than what most people, even veteran coaches, think—and even more vital.

Self-Awareness does not usually come easily. In fact, it often involves someone taking a hard look at your life and your choices in order to truly discover who you are. This was definitely the case for Dara Nielsen, Lead Engineer and Segment Manager for Lucas Systems, Inc.

On Dara's first day of her PEER Group Coaching experience, she was pretty skeptical, to say the least. She had no idea what to expect, and very little idea why she was even there. Dara had no clue that the next nine months would change her life, both personally and professionally. But midway through the Launch session, her attitude changed. As I shared earlier, participants are asked to define what they want their individual Outcome to be. Dara determined that she wanted to gain confidence in herself, to build a network of strong powerful peers to help support her, and to support them in turn. Yes, that all happened, but it went so much further.

For Dara, the hardest activity she encountered was "I Am From History." Because this task is a lesson in vulnerability for each person, inviting them to pause and reflect on the good, bad, and ugly of life to date, it is really an opportunity for people to exercise authentic Self-Awareness. By bravely reflecting on her life and facing some hard truths, Dara made a life-changing realization and adopted a new way of life. Her life shift was a pretty big one, as she found the courage to admit, both to herself and to the world, that she is bisexual.

The Self-Awareness that happened within that safe space taught Dara that it is completely acceptable to be vulnerable in ways most wouldn't dream of. She learned how to be vulnerable and discovered the power of it. With vulnerability comes courage. The courage she gained from hearing others share their experiences, and the support she felt when she shared hers, was incomparable to anything she had ever felt before. Dara discovered her true self, and was forever changed in the process.

> Since starting my PEER experience, Christy has instilled in me the confidence to ask for what I need, whether that's support from my Coaching Triad, to share a win with my cohort, or to tell my boss that I need a team of people to sustain the work I shouldered for a long time. Each time I attend a session or meet with my Triad, I leave feeling empowered to think deeply about what I want and pursue it. This is a huge mindset shift for me and one that has already paid dividends.
>
> **—Jackie Cappucci,**
> *Americas Marketing Manager, Industrial Scientific Corp.*

PEER Group Coaching teaches people the power of words, to truly know and find the voice to ask for what they want at work and at home. For Dara, it taught her how to be a strong, powerful woman in the male-dominated field of technology.

It also taught her how to define and set boundaries and how incredibly powerful (and liberating) it is to be vulnerable. The dynamic came from knowing that every one of these amazing leaders had her back and would never judge her. That is the Container in action as it shows people that it is completely acceptable to be vulnerable.

The EDGE experience also had hugely positive effects on Dara professionally. She became more confident as she gave herself permission to use her voice to share her opinion, perspective, and ideas. After learning from her peer group experience that language is generative and she is the author of her story, she became more deliberate, not only in what she said externally, but in her self-talk as well. Her leadership team couldn't help but see the changes in Dara. Soon afterwards, she received a huge promotion. Now, Dara leads an entirely new segment of the company, all because her Self-Awareness ignited a storm of possibility.

THE REAL STRATEGY

When healthy Self-Awareness is at work, the coach's role is to walk beside the cohort member as a companion, not to push or pull, as that person identifies their own authentic individual Outcomes. What's important in PEER Group Coaching is walking *beside* them, not in front of them (that is consulting), even if you've walked this path thousands of times.

But a basic paradox exists—we can't have Self-Awareness without first having Self-Awareness. Because if you don't have Self-Awareness, you can't have anything else. Once the Container is built, a safe space is created, but in order for anything to develop within the Container, we need Self-Awareness.

In addition, the arrows at the top indicate that Self-Awareness is where both learning (internal, in arrow) and growth (external, out arrow) take place for all the other elements. It is the gateway layer.

When I started to dig into why Self-Awareness is important and what exactly it is within the group coaching arena, I developed a strategy to increase it, in both participants and the coach. I call it REAL, which stands for Reflect, Engage, Apply, and Learn.

This strategy enables us to see how a coach holds the space for the group, and how that differs from 1:1 Coaching between two individuals. After all, as coaches, we are also on our own Self-Awareness journey. The minute we start acting like we know the *only* right way, we step out of our own Self-Awareness and lose focus on creating space and learning beside it. Just like with vulnerability, we too must model Self-Awareness in the group coaching context.

The REAL strategy has four steps used in every session of the PEER Group Coaching process. No matter how long or short the session. No matter what the dynamic. No matter which type of peer group. It always applies. And it always works.

1. Reflect.

When we reflect, we get curious. Through reflection, we help each person capture the essence of themselves. *What do I do? How do I do it? What's working? What's not?* Curiosity questions what we know and understand, even about Self-Awareness. There's no judgment with curiosity—it just is what is. For this reason, I intentionally included the Thought Spark questions at the end of each chapter. Vulnerability is the foundation of curiosity, and curiosity is the vehicle for innovation.

"Curiosity questions what we know and understand, even about Self-Awareness."

Throughout the PEER Framework, it is crucial to build in time for reflection and introspection. I suggest always having thoughtful pre-work, like an article or a video clip (keep five minutes or less) with a simple reflective worksheet that gets people digging in even before they arrive. I also always have some type of post-work. Even though the experience may be valuable at the moment, coaching is always about the application of learning. That reflection is needed on the back end, too.

I truly enjoyed meeting all the different women in various fields and seeing the progress over the 2-day Jumpstart experience. But interestingly for me, a very small but major thing had the biggest impact. There was one exercise where we wrote on sticky notes all the negative verbiage we speak to ourselves and then posted them on a wall. Hearing the statements read out loud and knowing I've spoken some of those very things or even thought them about myself—it was life changing for me. I believe life and death is in the power of the tongue, and I was immediately convicted about how I'd spoken to myself. Although the exercise may appear minor for some, it truly helped to change my mindset.

—Gabrielle Haywood,
Founder/CVO, Virginia Dere, LLC

2. Engage.

To engage requires two parts—*challenge* and *commitment*. Both are necessary. This understanding should remind most coaches of what we learned about 1:1 Coaching in coaching school. *Challenge* sounds like this: "This is how I'm showing up. I don't like the impact it is having in my life so much. How do I want to change?" *Commitment* happens when the person is ready to be coached. Desire for change has to come from the individual. In the PEER Group Coaching Framework, it's called *individual Outcomes. How do I want to be different in the future? What could change for me? How?*

In our longer EDGE group coaching experience, we can use different activities, similar to intake in 1:1 Coaching, to help cohort members engage. As the coach, we endeavor to create a space for them to see their future selves clearly. The first activity is to define their Outcome and envision the future. The second is to engage in some personal strategic planning on exactly how they plan to accomplish that outcome.

Once cohort members have identified their Outcomes, invite them to pull out their journals and continue the engagement through curiosity and reflect::

- ▶ **STOP:** How are you getting in your own way? What can you stop doing?
- ▶ **START:** What are you not doing now that, if you began, would help?
- ▶ **DO MORE OF:** What are you doing now that is working and that could do more often? How could you amplify it?
- ▶ **DO LESS OF:** If it is not realistic to totally stop doing it, what could you do less of?

"The PEER group coaching dynamic is something that did so much for me personally while providing the platform for each member to show vulnerability and support. I participated in an all-male cohort; not only, all-male but an 'alpha type' construction industry all-male cohort. Barriers were broken, trust was earned, and a 'Band of Brothers' was formed. Throughout this journey, I was challenged to dig deep and go somewhere I had never allowed myself to go.

I spent a lot of time in reflection and allowed myself the time for introspection. This was foreign to me. In this unfamiliar territory and with Christy's guidance I learned WHO I was, WHY I was this person, and WHAT I wanted to do with my God-given competencies and the skills developed along my journey. Through many insightful exercises and interactions throughout our group coaching experience. I was able to identify my core values and use them as the foundation to define my purpose and my vision. I created my mission statement, and this guides me no matter where I am in my career or in my life. "

—Chris Courson,

DPR Construction

3. Apply.

Once the foundation of curiosity is laid and members have begun to challenge that curiosity and commit to changing something in their lives right now, it's all about the application of new knowledge. Good coaches don't look at action steps. Instead, we embrace the imperfection that is, and look to integrate new practices with the goal to live a more fulfilled life.

> The PEER experience allowed me to hone my sense of self. It afforded me the guidance and space to define my personal goals, life anchors, and core values, uninhibited by others' standards or expectations of me. This allowed me to recognize personal attributes that I had previously shied away from as essential elements of my personal brand. The experience also gave me the encouragement and courage to present that brand to the world. Truly understanding my core values has allowed me to interpret my own emotions and to understand and set personal boundaries more effectively.
>
> **—Allison Schlaegle,**
> *Director, Marketing Strategy, Highmark Health*

We do this in PEER Group Coaching by employing Accountability Partners and Coaching Triads (more details on these later) to integrate practice in the magical *in-between time* of monthly sessions across the longer group coaching experience. For the concentrated Ignite, THRIVE, and Jumpstart experiences, we invite people to engage with one another after the session to serve in the role of Accountability Partners.

In these experiences, we randomly place people into pairs at the close of each session and invite them to share their Outcomes and first steps with the other person. Then we create intentional space to receive feedback and insight from that peer on best practices. Each person leaves the interaction with a commitment to make that first step and a partner to hold them accountable. This accountability could be as simple as Regina asking Chantelle to follow up with a quick call, text, or email in two weeks.

This Apply step also points to another huge difference between traditional training and PEER Group Coaching. The latter focuses less on information and more on knowledge. It might help to think of the difference between the two as an image made with a cluster of dots. Each dot represents information that is critical to success. But until the dots are connected (or applied) the dots are just that—dots. The connections create the knowledge pathways to change and transformation when Regina follows up and coaches Chantelle: *What did you try? What worked? What didn't work so much? Why do you think that is? Where do you want to go from there? How can I be a good accountability partner for you as you take this first step?*

4. Learn.

After someone has practiced and applied a new choice, the stage is set for growth to learn from it. This is where we support our cohort members to help one another get curious about the results, the emotional underpinnings, and the language being used. Cohort members take those great coaching questions their peers asked them and evaluate their actions and self-talk to learn from it. Then the cycle repeats as they circle back around to Step 1 and re-Reflect on the learning, become more Engaged, Apply, and Learn.

As coaches we know (in our Belly) that Self-Awareness is not static. It does not exist in a vacuum. Self-Awareness evolves as each individual evolves. As the individual evolves, the group evolves. Then the entire organization evolves. And then the world. That's the power of the dynamic experience to develop and maintain a healthy sense of Self-Awareness, both individually and as part of a larger whole. It's not about deciding what a person will or won't do, because we are all co-creating the direction of this group coaching experience together with an equal voice. There are both similarities and differences in individual Outcomes. It's not *either/or*, but *both/and*. Everybody's got their own thing, *and* we're all in it together.

"Self-awareness evolves as each individual evolves. As the individual evolves, the group evolves. Then the entire organization evolves. And then the world."

The reality is, we all have a lot in common. Our shared stories heighten our Self-Awareness, help us reflect, and invite us to get curious. We write all sorts of stories in our minds (like my opening story in Chapter 1) without being aware of them, until we get curious about what we're doing and how we're showing up. It's not enough simply to ask questions and reflect. We have to find the answers, apply new practices, embrace imperfection, and generate growth.

My PEER experience gave me pause to think about me, and me alone. It allowed me to take inventory of who I was, who I have become and where I really wanted to go. The experience took me through true reflection that allowed me to identify baggage and inner critic messages that were not allowing me to be truly happy or motivated or courageous with my talents. It also helped me get back to my value system which has changed as my life circumstances have changed. The group coaching experience exposed me to other women who shared, listened and encouraged me to dream and know my value and what I bring to my family and my work. EDGE gave me a support group to bring my toughest problems to and ask for support. It gave me roots, a vision and a group of supporters like I've never had before.

—Grace Wirfel,
Manager of Leadership Development and Talent Management, Sheetz, Inc.

Coaches help participants ignite curiosity in one another, but there has to be some desire for change from the individual. It can't come from their boss. It can't come from the group. Truly great group coaching experiences create the space in the cohort where each individual can ask, *What do I want to get out of this? How do I want to be different nine months from now? What does success look like for me?* Then they can commit further and deeper by asking, *What can I let go of in order to get to where I want to go? What permission can I give myself?*

Remember that coaches also have a role by applying gentle irreverence and challenging each person's status quo. We may do it with kindness and patience, but we challenge each person nonetheless to push past initial roadblocks, frustrations, discomfort, and fear.

We will fail simply because we're beginners, and we will improve if we keep practicing. When practicing a new behavior, it's really like practicing a new choice. Ideally, there's some level of experiential learning in the practice, but that's where having an accountability partner comes into play. Someone else can help apply the learning and hold the cohort member accountable.

It's no surprise that once again, vulnerability comes front and center. It's a vulnerable act to commit to becoming more self-aware, trying something new, and asking someone for accountability. It's a vulnerable act to reflect on what worked well and to change behavior. It is a vulnerable act for someone to see oneself clearly with imperfections. It is a vulnerable act to give oneself permission to say something out loud, to be heard and seen in a group. It is a vulnerable act to change.

SELF-AWARENESS IN ACTION

I would love to introduce you to Keisha Pendleton. She heard about EDGE and decided to take part in one of my public cohorts in 2017 while working at Carlow University as a Project Manager. Keisha gave herself permission to engage in very deep conversations with her PEER group coaching cohort. She felt the energy was electrifying. Everyone became very vulnerable and opened up to one another as they co-created their Container and charted a course towards their Outcomes as a peer group.

As an African American woman, Keisha wanted to know how to gain confidence to effectively network in circles that didn't always look like her. When I met Keisha, I saw the bright flame within her, but I'm not so sure she did. She seemed to lack confidence within herself, perhaps because Keisha had been going through a rough patch in her life, both personally and professionally. She came to the cohort to learn from the others, but she had no idea she would end up contributing just as much (if not more) than she received. Over the course of 9 months, Keisha was able to give back and assist others who were currently shifting careers or redefining themselves in the workforce.

As their skill level and desire for Self-Awareness increased, Keisha's cohort began to extend the practice of our Vulnerability Levels (the roles of the Head, Heart, and Belly) in decision making and the way they processed life overall. She began to be sensitive to where decisions were being made: Was she thinking with her Head, being very analytical and logical? Was she feeling triggered by emotions going on in the Heart? Or, was she being guided by the intuition of the Belly? Listening to everyone tell their stories and tapping into the PEER Vulnerability Levels helped Keisha take a hard look at how she was interpreting her role in the world and, most importantly, how and where she wanted to shift it.

As a result of the increased Self-Awareness, Keisha learned that holding each other accountable, asking for support, and sharing successes is powerful and life changing. She truly benefited from having an accountability partner, knowing that someone else was going to check up on her personal and professional goals each month as she charted her course towards her individual EDGE Outcome. This level of expectation helped Keisha powerfully shift her priorities. For example, if she wanted to exercise, but didn't feel as though she had the time, the accountability partner would consistently follow up and hold her accountable.

She was able to develop the confidence she needed. After completing the PEER group coaching experience, as she would proudly tell you today, she became a new woman. Being part of it provided Keisha with an enormous number of resources and gave her the opportunity to connect with many great leaders.

Within five months of graduating from EDGE, she was promoted into a position she had wanted for some time. For Keisha, it was all about having the confidence within herself that she knows what she is doing and deserves to have a seat at the table. Two years later, in 2019, she was promoted again and relocated into a new industry and a new state. Although she is the only non-white person on her project, she finds the position rewarding. She was able to implement all the tools acquired through the PEER group and to maintain the relationships with the other women in her cohort several years later.

A gentle reminder: it's important to remember that it is not our job as a coach to fix people. It's our job to walk beside somebody on their journey. We don't tell someone like Keisha, "Hey, you've got a stone in your shoe." Instead, what we do is get curious: "I'm noticing that you're limping, Keisha. What could it look like if we stopped walking? Let's sit together for a minute. Tell me about what's going on." We're always trying to fan the flames of their Self-Awareness.

Once someone exercises Self-Awareness to identify individual Outcomes, they're going to apply this REAL process again and again. That is why no matter the dynamics of the group or the time frame in which they meet, cohort members cycle through this REAL strategy every single time. Group coaching is about *connection, contribution,* and *community*—all of which require authentic Self-Awareness to flourish.

IGNITE: BEST PRACTICES

✓ Without the Container, we can't have Self-Awareness. Without Self-Awareness, we can't have anything else.

✓ Self-Awareness is the layer of the Framework through which learning and growth take place. Every other element depends on it.

✓ Within the context of the group coaching experience, people are encouraged to generate their own individual Outcomes, but authentic Self-Awareness is necessary as the first step.

✓ My strategy to increase Self-Awareness in both participants and us as the group coach, called REAL, stands for Reflect, Engage, Apply, and Learn.

- **Reflect.** When we reflect, we get curious. Through reflection, we help each person capture the essence of themselves in that exact moment of evolution. Vulnerability is the foundation of curiosity, and curiosity is the vehicle for innovation.

- **Engage.** To engage requires two parts—*challenge* and *commitment*. *Challenge* is how someone is showing up, and identifying where and when they don't like the impact something is having in their life. *Commitment* happens when the person is ready to shift behaviors and to be coached. Desire for change has to come from the individual.

- **Apply.** We embrace the imperfection that is, and look to integrate new practices. We do this in PEER Group Coaching by employing Accountability Partners and Coaching Triads to integrate practice in the magical *in-between time* of monthly sessions for longer group coaching experiences like EDGE.

- **Learn.** This is where we support our cohort members to help one another get curious about the results, the emotional underpinnings, and the language being used to make sense of it all.

✓ Once someone exercises Self-Awareness to identify individual Outcomes, they're going to apply this REAL process again and again. It is circular, not linear.

THOUGHT SPARKS

1. *Think of a time where Self-Awareness allowed you to shift in a powerful way personally or professionally. What ignited it for you? What did you choose to change? How?*

2. *In your life right now, where do you feel stuck? Why? What would you change if you could?*

3. *How do you encourage Self-Awareness in your current coaching practice or leadership style? What works well? What doesn't?*

4. *How could you model Self-Awareness in a group coaching experience?*

5. *Can you think of a situation where having an accountability partner helped you stay on target? What was most valuable about this for you? Why?*

6. *Can you think of a time when you tried to coach someone who was not ready for it? How do you know when someone is ready to deepen their Self-Awareness?*

OUTCOMES

*"Traveler, there is no road; you make
your own path as you walk."*

—ANTONIO MACHADO

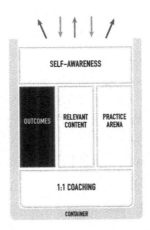

B efore you begin any journey, it's important to know where you're going. When it comes to PEER Group Coaching, the coach needs to ask what *both* the organization or peer group *and* the individual cohort members truly want out of the experience.

Why are *they* buying into this development opportunity? What are the Outcomes *they* desire?

In 1:1 Coaching, we do this in the initial intake session because identifying Outcomes is really like goal setting, and goal setting is the mortar in the foundation of all coaching. At the start of any PEER experience, no matter the duration,

"Outcomes are the return on investment." it is vital to find out what Outcomes determine success for them. As any good coach knows, we need have to ask how the cohort member wants to be different after the experience. What is their

desired impact? What about for the organization and/or larger peer group as a whole? How do they desire to be different? The bottom line is, Outcomes are the return on investment. And it is up to the group coach to help everyone define their unique ROI.

Sometimes the Outcomes uncovered may be unexpected or not based solely on professional goals, just like we often see in our private coaching practice with individuals. But because they are still incredibly powerful, they affect professional performance. For example, when Jodi Liscio joined one of my EDGE cohorts, I asked this question as part of the Container building process in the Launch session: *What would you do if you had no fear?* When Jodi heard those words, her Self-Awareness told her she already knew the answer, even though she couldn't bring herself to share out loud yet.

You see, Jodi was a successful VP who had become perfect at living a hollow life. She felt like she couldn't find joy in anything anymore, except loving her child. From intense marriage and family difficulties to serious health challenges to having been a victim of violent crime, Jodi had endured a great deal coming into her group coaching experience. Yet, if you looked at Jodi, you would think she had it all. She lived in a beautiful house she had designed herself in one of the best neighborhoods. The house was featured in her city's annual Parade of Homes Tour. She drove a BMW convertible, attended charity events, and always showed up at work confident and powerful. She was perceived as being bold and unrelenting, a strong and confident woman.

But the truth was, Jodi was haunted every day by the vapid reality of her life. She was living a life that felt empty, but she wasn't ready to be vulnerable, or even to tell her best friends about it yet. Every day she felt as if she were drowning a little more. What she knew deep down in that Launch session, even though she could not bring herself to verbalize it yet, was that without fear, she would change three things in her life: separate from her husband, transition to meaningful work, and live boldly and bravely.

She wanted to do the personal work necessary to overcome her life's trauma. She wanted to get as mentally and physically healthy as possible to be an ideal role model for her child. She sat in that room knowing she was living a slow, progressing march towards death if she didn't find the courage to change.

IT'S TIME TO GET PERSONAL

Understanding individual Outcomes is key, but as a coach, you also have to think about organizational Outcomes. After all, the corporation is the paying client behind all of the personal growth. It behooves us to pay very, very close attention to them. You need to find out what the company is looking to shift, improve, or change (remember back to our story with Sheetz and their Outcomes for their front-line leaders). Once you understand the company's goals, then you create space in your group coaching experience to invite each member to reflect and explore their own individual Outcomes.

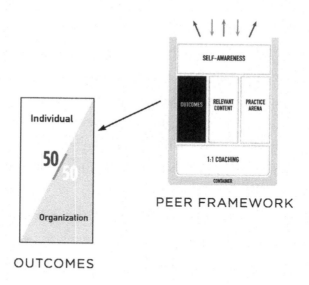

OUTCOMES   PEER FRAMEWORK

By discovering the company, the peer group, and the individual Outcomes, you can tailor the PEER group experience just as you would customize a 1:1 Coaching engagement. But as important as it is to understand everyone's Outcomes, remember that not everyone is ready to share them. Like Jodi, they may need time, either to become self-aware or to build trust so they can practice the skill of vulnerability to speak the words—and the possibilities—out loud. Many introverts (like me) can feel overwhelmed or even exposed by being put on the spot. As a result, some people might initially resist declaring the person they want to be nine months down the road.

The PEER Framework gives leaders the ability to connect with their team in a new way to connect with the whole person, not just their work performance. In thinking about dynamic management teams, having that connection not only with their work related output but them as a person helps demonstrate genuine care, that you want to help them and be there for them. This is the type of culture we are trying to create as leaders. There is a genuine nature that comes through in Christy's group coaching experience. I've dealt with other facilitators and coaches before, and I can tell you, this is a different approach.

—Todd W. Faulk,
Vice President of Human Resources, Duquesne Light Company

On the other hand, a lot of people simply do not know what they want because they haven't taken the time to truly reflect on themselves. Perhaps they've been focused on satisfying someone else's expectations, caring for others, or trying to achieve what they think their life and career goals should look like. As a result, great group coaches can flex with each cohort depending on their needs.

Some groups (or individuals) will simply need more time to work through this process of identifying Outcomes as you help them pull back the layers. That's why it's important to give time for participants to feel comfortable and to create a safe Container in which they can practice vulnerability. Give them the space to sit and think freely so they can discover a better Outcome that really works for them. You can do this by building reflection and outcome-setting time into the agenda of a longer group coaching experience that is at least two days long. In fact, in a 6-month session, for example, we give members four weeks to determine their Outcomes. In a 9-month EDGE experience, it could take up to six weeks. We also expect those Outcomes to shift for about a third of the members throughout the experience, just like they would for a 1:1 Coaching engagement.

When we deliver the extended EDGE group experience, we encourage participants to explore and connect to their Outcomes at the Launch, Midpoint, and Continuation. This revisiting helps participants identify deeper parts of their individual Outcomes and authentically look for meaningful connections to what the company wants them to get out of it, how they want to be different in their lives, and what they need to do to show up more confidently. Many people achieve their initial Outcomes by the Midpoint. They may realize they are now really ready to go deeper as Relevant Content (Chapter 9) helps them redefine, and a dynamic Self-Awareness sparks them to realign their priorities. We always plan intentional time in the schedule for the longer sessions to allow for this adjustment to take place. In fact, for most of the remainder of this chapter, I'll be addressing how to identify Outcomes for the longer sessions where more time is available to go deeper with members.

THE PROCESS OF IDENTIFYING OUTCOMES

When launching longer group coaching experiences like EDGE, setting up the Outcomes as a continuous journey is especially important because you'll revisit the Outcomes again and again throughout both the group journey and in 1:1 Coaching. I've found coaches need to prime the pump, so to speak, and frontload the experience with a series of experiential learning (EXL) activities while the Container is still being built in months one and two. These activities get participants envisioning the person and leader they want to be at the end of the experience.

Creative activities are essential to identifying Outcomes. We want to get members out of their left brain and into their right brain. In EDGE we use a vision-boarding activity to do that. Sometimes before people have the words, they can have the picture. We supply them with a Launch box filled with materials for creative expression and motivational quotes.

The thing to realize is, people often get frustrated when trying to figure out what their Outcomes are. On the surface, at least, they often have numerous excuses and objections as to why they don't or can't know what their Outcomes might be. It's almost as if we have to help them sneak up on themselves, because, as the Jodi example shows, they really do know what the Outcomes are, but haven't taken the time to clarify them in the busyness of living life, or have lacked the courage to express them (even to themselves).

> *"People often get frustrated when trying to figure out what their Outcomes are."*

For the corporate audience, I recommend you do not call it a Vision Board, and instead focus on introspection, which I often refer to as Personal Strategic Planning. Begin by asking them to consider some key questions in three domains: career, personal, and community. You can customize these for whatever domains are relevant to your group:

- ▶ Think about the leader you want to be at work nine months from now. What are you doing? What are you not doing?
- ▶ Think about your desired personal life nine months from now. What are you doing? What are you not doing?
- ▶ Think about how you want to show up in your community nine months from now. What are you doing? What are you not doing?

Then, we invite them to use all the creative expression supplies we gave them in their Launch box to customize a folder that answers those questions for them. For virtual sessions, they can draw from other items they have in their home, as well. We give them the choice of working together with others or alone for about 30-45 minutes to complete the activity. As a general rule, I have found women take longer than men to complete this activity. That is not a reflection of creativity levels in any way, but something to keep in mind when budgeting time in the experience. When they come back to the group, each person has the opportunity to share their folder. For virtual sessions, they hold it up to the camera and can choose to what extent they want to explain what they did and why. Some people keep it simple. Others decorate the front, back, and even the inside. But whatever they choose has powerful meaning.

We do this creative activity because if we were to simply ask people what their Outcomes were, they might struggle and become frustrated. But if we lead them through this process, not only do they get more clarity about their own Outcomes, they practice intentional vulnerability and connections and relationships grow as they are often inspired by a quote or image someone else shares, as well. This is a very simple way to model for them the value of being a part of a peer group, right off the bat in the Launch.

In EDGE, we give members four to six weeks to clarify their Outcomes and send them to the coach. But knowing the answers to these questions can be challenging. That is why we, as coaches, must intentionally build thoughtful conversations into the experience both prior to and after this activity to begin to uncover and unfold these individual Outcomes.

No matter the length of the PEER Group Coaching experience, we find people need to first reflect on where they have been to then determine where they are. That is why the "I Am From History" activity can be so useful. Creating the space to open up and share these histories is usually one of the most powerful parts of our Launch. Once they can clearly see where they have been—with both the light and the shadow sides—they can better determine where they want to go next.

As such, Day One of the Launch is usually reflective at first, talking through where they are right now, usually in a series of small group conversations that leave them feeling more connected to peers and knowing they are not alone.

"We only change when the pain of staying the same is greater than the pain of changing."

That might involve discussing questions about context, like, "What does your perfect day look like?" One I used a lot after the COVID pandemic lockdowns was, "What was the hardest part of the lockdown for you? Why?" The questions can and should adjust based on audience, circumstance, and setting. Remember, the value of group coaching is in the peer group, so these conversations must happen amongst the group, not with you.

Just like any good intake session in a 1:1 Coaching engagement, we need to create space every month for each person to explore how they are feeling at that moment. Because we only change when the pain of staying the same is greater than the pain of changing.

DYNAMIC OUTCOMES

The Outcomes members set get revisited throughout the PEER Group Coaching experience. They get revisited every single month in the Mastermind, which we'll discuss in Chapter 10, in the Coaching Triads, and in Office Hours (Chapter 11). They are woven throughout the entire experience and everything ties to them. *Outcomes are at the heart of every single element of the PEER Group Coaching Framework.*

I have applied concepts that I learned in my PEER experience that led to a renewed focus on my professional growth. This included knowing that being authentically me is always the best "me" to bring to work and life. I have real value that I contribute, and a perspective that is worth acknowledging. There is power in being myself and doing what serves me as a priority.

—Lauren Barrish,

Manager

Once cohort members establish their individual Outcomes, they can develop their ideal strategy in several ways. For longer group coaching experiences, we offer Office Hours where members can choose to schedule 1:1 Coaching time with the group coach to get direct support. Throughout the experience, they also get help within their monthly Coaching Triad (more on those shortly) to develop the best possible next steps for their success.

As coaches, it's up to us to be super clear about the Outcomes for our group coaching strategy. To that end, customizing the Outcomes to fit the needs of the organization is key, but it is not enough. After all, PEER Group Coaching is *not* a training program. Group coaching should never take a cookie cutter approach. It's designed to meet both the needs of each person and of the organization. And because every cohort is made up of different individuals, it is never the same twice. For example, at one Fortune 50 company we work with, we've had nearly twenty EDGE cohorts at the time of this writing. Even though the structure of the group coaching experience has been identical, every single cohort was different because the value is in the richness of the unique dialogue each person brings and shares.

When she first set her Outcomes, Jodi Liscio couldn't bring herself to say what she knew deep down she really wanted. What she gradually came to realize through the experience was she only needed to figure out how to take one first step—one small step of change—and slowly her light would grow and flourish.

Over time, Jodi came to realize her core Outcome was to love herself again. It was to believe she was enough for herself, and she did not need to pretend any longer. The PEER group experience gave her the courage to continue to experience the REAL Self-Awareness cycle and engage and identify with what she really wanted.

Jodi finally had the courage to be "ALL IN" only after the 9-month cohort was completed. In fact, her moment of clarity came in the middle of the night when, in a courageous moment of Self-Awareness, she finally decided to be "ALL IN" for her own Outcomes. She was able to separate from her husband and successfully stand on her own. She learned to love herself again. She adjusted her internal dialogue to use healthier language. She started being present in her life and writing a better story for herself.

Professionally, Jodi began leading and mentoring women inside her company and in her community. She networked with executives and found ways to give back to charity. She paid it forward by spending time with women around her organization, understanding their challenges, and becoming a voice for them. She began thriving by empowering her entire amazing team to step into their own light and shine. Since the PEER Group Coaching experience, Jodi is healthier, happier, and more whole than she has been in her entire life. She is finally living her own version of success.

We often hear stories like Jodi's of how their group coaching experience has changed their lives, but in reality, it is the members who actually make the seismic life shifts that help them ultimately achieve their Outcomes. The coach's role in the PEER Framework is to give them the space to do it thoughtfully and well, all in a Container that evolves alongside their own growing Self-Awareness. Only then, when Outcomes are identified, both within the organization and with each individual, is it time to bring Relevant Content into the experience in an innovative and powerful way.

IGNITE BEST PRACTICES

✓ It's important to have a clear idea of individual Outcomes as well as organizational Outcomes. They are equally important.

✓ By discovering the company, the peer group, and the individual Outcomes, you can tailor the experience just as you would customize a 1:1 Coaching engagement.

✓ Build reflection and Outcome-setting time into the agenda of any group coaching experience that is at least two days long. In a 9-month EDGE experience, it could take up to six weeks. Be patient.

✓ During any longer PEER group experience, encourage participants to explore and purposefully connect to their Outcomes at the Launch, Midpoint, and Continuation.

✓ Creative activities are essential to identifying Outcomes. We often use a vision-boarding activity to do that. Sometimes before people have the words, they can have the picture.

✓ Once individual Outcomes are established, offer Office Hours and Triad Coaching to help them develop the best strategy for success. Cohort members can choose to schedule 1:1 Coaching time to get direct support from the group coach as well.

✓ Group coaching is dynamic and should never take a cookie cutter approach. It's designed to meet both the needs of each person and of the organization and must evolve as they do.

✓ The coach's role is to walk beside each cohort member as a companion as they identify their own authentic individual. Outcomes, not to push or pull someone. We companion.

THOUGHT SPARKS

1. *What really resonated about Outcome setting for you? Why?*

2. *How effectively do you help people identify personal or professional Outcomes in your current coaching model? What works well for you? What could be stronger?*

3. I mention creating a vision board as an activity to help people identify Outcomes. What other types of right-brain activities could you use to help cohort members "back into" their Outcomes?

4. Have you identified your Outcomes in reading this book? What does success look like for you? (Example: You know your investment of time was worthwhile if, at the end of reading, you nowreading, you now _____ _____.)

Tip for Concentrated Experiences

For shorter 1-2 hour Ignite Coaching Circles, or even a 2-day Jumpstart session, I recommend creating reflective ppre-work to better support your Outcome-setting process, so people can come into it with more clarity about what they want. We often use an online survey to gather data in advance of these shorter sessions so we can adjust the Relevant Content to the audience, maximize the group coaching experience, and use their own words to describe the Outcomes for the group coaching experience.

This pre-knowledge also allows the coach to share the Outcomes at the start of the session—what will be covered and what will not be—so no one leaves disappointed. (I also recommend including session Outcomes in the marketing of all experiences so the stage is clearly set when people enroll.)

9

RELEVANT CONTENT

"In learning you will teach, and in teaching you will learn."

—PHIL COLLINS

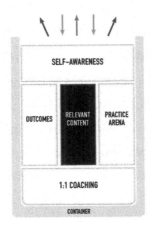

Relevant Content is a small but mighty part of the PEER Group Coaching Framework. In its essence, Relevant Content is central to it, and yet, the content takes up only about 10% of the experience. But that 10% is critical.

In the PEER experience, the choice of content should be directly driven by both the organizational and cohort members' Outcomes. So when choosing content, make sure it is relevant to both parties. Always ask why people are investing in the experience and what they want to learn. In my coaching practice, organizational Outcomes drive around 85% of the content. After all, it is the organization that's paying for the experience.

There are two aspects to this content element in the PEER Group Coaching Framework and each delivers about 50% of the value. The first is content that you, as the coach, bring based on research and data. These could be from books, articles, worksheets, and studies. This is the only time you could be seen as the "expert" in this group coaching experience. The second is to create the space for vertical knowledge transfer. This is where you fall back into your role as facilitator for discussions or, my favorite, inviting Guest Mentors. You can bring in Guest Mentors to share experiences and best practices around the content co-created by the cohort, and in doing so, turn the role of "expert" over once again.

The former is purely driven from organizational Outcomes. It will stay the same across multiple cohorts inside the same company. This is important because the company is investing in this group coaching experience to move the needle in some important way. Ideally, you will dive into these competencies alongside HR and L&D to ensure what you build is thoughtfully aligned.

The first 50% of Relevant Content is what you as a coach curate. When choosing Relevant Content for a group, I suggest at least two, but no more than four, content competencies or areas. Regardless of what you choose, and no matter the group, the first content area should always be coaching, because it is central to the entire process. You have to teach cohort members Coaching skills for them to peer coach one another. Next, pick other content areas. I prefer three content areas for my groups in the extended program, EDGE.

Within my high-potential, co-ed leadership groups, the choices are usually Coaching, Personal Branding, and some type of Influence-related topic, because this is where the research shows gaps for early and mid-career leaders within typical organizations. I will use them as examples in this chapter so you can see how I apply Relevant Content, but remember that you can choose whatever content is deemed relevant for your audience, clients, and practice.

First, Coaching is an incredibly transferable skill. It holds value for managers and individual contributors alike, so regardless of the peer group type, they will immediately be able to put it into use at work. We layer coaching into every single PEER Group Coaching experience, from early career cohorts onboarding fresh college grads to C-suite executive peer groups. Everyone gains value from it as a skill because the power of a peer group is in creating the space for each person to become a mirror to one another. It also brings value to personal lives, as we coaches know better than most. We can coach our peers on nonprofit boards, our siblings, parents, teenagers, sometimes even (if we are careful) our partners and spouses!

Second, Personal Brand is about asking, "Who am I as a leader? What is important to me? What is the impact I want to have at work? In the community? At home?" Personal Brand is not self promotion. It is delving deep into Self-Awareness and identifying our personal leadership core values, our purpose and vision. It is about creating a clear path forward with accountability in how you want to show up, and living authentically in that manner daily.

With some of my clients, we often tie this portion of the content to the Leadership Standards for the company. For example, I have a company I work with in the utility industry who is focused on a culture change to include the competency of empathy. For them, we layered the skill of empathy into both coaching and personal branding by supporting the cohort members in identifying how the concept aligns with who they are and finding their own personal version of how to apply the skill. At this company, we first began with group coaching a cohort of officers, then cascaded our PEER Framework throughout every level of people leaders.

Influence-related topics could include exploring questions such as:

- ► In what domain do I want to concentrate and build my strategic network right now? Internal? External? The Community?
- ► Why does this feel important to me this year?
- ► How will doing so help me achieve my individual Outcomes?

> The personal branding content had a tremendous impact on me. This exercise helped me realize what I viewed as weakness in my character others admired and saw as strengths. I learned that I was in fact consistently living my personal brand both personally and professionally, and this was a game changer for me. This gave me the confidence I needed to speak up more in meetings and volunteer for tasks that I would not have otherwise stepped up to take on. Now, as I am mentoring other women, I am aware of the importance of challenging them to see their value and strengths and write their own story. This is my way to pay-it-forward and continue to give back to the network of women who have been so supportive of me.
>
> **—Rose Kopp,**
> *Chief of Staff to AMG CIO, PNC Financial Services*

The content competencies you select should also align with your experience and expertise. I selected Coaching, Personal Brand, and Influence because the research shows it meets a need in my client base, *and* because I personally have seen the impact deploying them can bring. The power lies in how "relevant" the content is to your cohort. For example, a topic could be around acquiring more influence or leveraging what they have. It could be customized around change management in a company undergoing a new strategic shift or merger. It could be how to become an advocate or ally for others seeking to rise within the organization. Again, what is most important is that the Relevant Content areas be tied to the organizational Outcomes for your client. What change do they want to create within this peer group? What behaviors do they want to see shifted in their participants? What is their return on investment? In that way, the topics can always shift because your content has to be relevant to the audience and firmly attached to Outcomes.

MAKING IT MAKE SENSE

My very first group cohort was with working moms when it launched in 2007. To be honest, it simply was not sustainable. Why? It was missing the key component—Relevant Content. If I could do it all over again, I would integrate thoughtful content throughout my early group coaching experiences. Even though I didn't have the resources then to create worksheets and materials, we could have used articles or a podcast to give us action nuggets to discuss and put to use in our lives. We could have used it to hold one another accountable to apply and practice content from previous sessions together, sharing insights we learned.

Without Relevant Content, the sessions could only be based on the ebbs and flows of the challenges each peer brought to our monthly Mastermind sessions (Chapter 10).. The problem with that was it would often turn into a complaint fest. We early cohort members would often just talk about our problems without access to real solutions. Our singular focus was around best practices sharing (because I hadn't yet even thought of the concept of peer coaching!).

I quickly realized we needed to introduce targeted content relevant to the group to make the magic happen. Without it, there were limits to what could be done. A peer group always risks running out of knowledge because we simply do not know what we do not know. In order to keep the learning flowing, there has to be a spring of content coming in to nourish the new growth. So we all began to layer in articles and books the group could discuss. As a L&D professional, I began to create reflective worksheets the cohort members could use to apply their learnings.

But it still wasn't enough. We needed the other 50% of Relevant Content to come from outside sources which came to be called Guest Mentors.

The idea for layering in Guest Mentors came about two years later in 2009 during my second attempt at group coaching. This time it was with a cohort of high-potential women leaders across companies and industries. As I was discussing the need for what I later termed *vertical knowledge transfer* with one of my mentors, Aradhna Dhanda-Oliphant, she asked if I had ever thought about bringing in guest speakers. I initially shot down her suggestion because I didn't want someone standing at a lectern talking at people for ninety minutes, simply spewing content. I wanted it to be a dialogue that would help cohort members discuss the topics that mattered most to them, hear the best practices and lessons learned about those topics, and then to apply what they learn.

Always leading with innovation, Aradhna challenged me further. Through that conversation of possibility, we came up with the idea of bringing in Guest Mentors. Living her personal purpose to connect people and ideas together, she generously offered to help fill our cohort's pipeline with talented folks from the Pittsburgh area to beta test the idea, and we were off and running. To this day, the Guest Mentor component is one of the most popular aspects of our PEER Group Coaching Framework. We layer it in not only with the longer EDGE experiences, but also with the 2-day Jumpstart. And I love that the idea was never mine to begin with! It is a vehicle for vertical knowledge transfer, and it came organically from my mentor doing just that.

Consider the experience of Bear Brandegee, ACC. In one way or another, Bear has been coaching her whole life, finding ways to help people show up in a powerful way. She started out in the marketing communications realm, then eventually moved into style and strategy. Having an MBA, a degree in English, and a background in fashion, Bear had a strong education and business background, but no formal coaching training.

I met Bear in 2018 when I invited her to be a Guest Mentor for one of my group coaching experiences. She would tell you it was the beginning of her formal coaching journey because she had always been in a role of working with senior executives and community leaders in various consulting, advisory, and coaching roles, but had never even heard of coaching "school."

So, when I met Bear, I asked if she had ever considered formal coaching certification because I could tell she was a natural coach. My question took Bear by surprise. She had never considered the idea. Once we talked about it more, however, Bear went to get ICF certified through New Ventures West, a school from which I often hire coaches.

When someone doesn't have a clear direction in life, they can have one foot on one path and the other foot on a different path. When Bear became certified as a coach, her direction became clear, and she felt completely centered with both feet on the same path. As a result, Bear started her own coaching business focused on both life and executive coaching.

"The PEER Group Coaching Framework is that it effectively pulls out the essential elements of coaching and repackages them in a scalable way within a corporate environment."

Within the PEER group coaching experience, the coach still has the opportunity to work 1:1 with each peer within a cohort, but coaching an individual is very different from coaching a group. However, given the intimacy and vulnerability of the experience, the coach can deliver the depth of 1:1 Coaching within a group setting.

What I love about the PEER Group Coaching Framework is that it effectively pulls out the essential elements of coaching and repackages them in a scalable way within a corporate environment. It is adjustable and relevant to each leader, each company, and each organization. For coaches interested in building a group coaching practice, the PEER Group Coaching Framework is a simple platform for any coach to use to expand their business. Because of its modular, plug-and-play nature, a coach could easily construct a curriculum based on their needs and craft a customized program with their own personal flavor to make it their own.

Eventually, I saw Bear would make a great fit for the PEER Group Coaching experience and offered her the opportunity to partner with us. Since she was used to coaching 1:1 with individuals, Bear found group coaching different and exciting and has been passionate about it ever since.

DIVERSE VOICES

One thing to note: you will want to introduce diversity of thought and experiences through these Guest Mentors in a thoughtful way to amplify your organizational Outcomes. For example, we have a 2-day Jumpstart for men where the Guest Mentors intentionally include women. These female Guest Mentors share experiences of the power of someone being an advocate and ally for them in their life to empower the cohort of men to see a different perspective and grow in those areas. As always, keep both the organizational and the individual Outcomes in mind as well as Relevant Content areas when considering whom to invite as a Guest Mentor.

As another example, we do a lot of high-potential women's leadership group coaching experiences with the goal of creating a sustainable pipeline of female talent to the officer level. When we work with Fortune 500 companies to source their Guest Mentors, we want them to be executives inside the company because one of the Outcomes is to build credibility and create greater visibility for their high-potential women. The Guest Mentor experience becomes an opportunity for them to have exposure to senior leaders to whom they might not normally have access. That, in turn, aligns with the Relevant Content of building (and leveraging) a personal brand, expanding influence via networking, and creating a space to meet potential advocates and mentors.

In these instances, I encourage organizations to bring in a mix of voices across the gender spectrum for different perspectives. When creating a pipeline of female talent is a goal, like we saw earlier with Sheetz, I encourage bringing in a C-level male leader whenever possible alongside a female executive. As they bond over content they are both passionate about, they also share best practices. He learns from her, she learns from him, and, just perhaps, an organic mentorship or sponsorship relationship can begin to bloom. Of course, I encourage you to mix it up in any way you choose. It just so happens more often than not that our clients in male-dominated industries have C-Suites that are mostly male and are looking to build a sustainable female talent pipeline.

PUTTING RELEVANT CONTENT TO WORK

How do you effectively incorporate Guest Mentors into the PEER experience? First, remember that while the first part of the Relevant Content is driven by the organizational Outcomes, this second part must be co-created by the peer group. I recommend offering a menu of topics from which the cohort can pick. When I work inside Fortune 500 companies, I offer the option of possible topics layered into a Guest Mentor Topic Menu. The L&D team can then customize based on their organizational Outcomes. Then, even though the cohort gets to select their three topics, they are selecting from a carefully curated list in which the company already sees as developmental areas based on their people data and analytics. The one best practice I would give is to always include a write-in portion on your Guest Mentor Topic Menu. Every once in a while, a topic is truly driven by the cohort themselves, and when they do, you can provide powerful insight back to your client about a new gap they may not have been aware of.

Once topics are chosen, the company (or the coach) can find executive leaders who are seasoned in those topics and have great stories to tell. These topics can be as wide-ranging as living an anti-racist life to learning how to let things go and not take them personally. They can be topics about embracing innovation, time management best practices, or organizational savvy. Depending on the organizational Outcomes, they can even be tradition-ally "hard skills," like reading balance sheets and financial state-ments. Again, all the topics should be aligned with the organi-zational Outcomes.

The Relevant Content in every one of our EDGE group coaching experiences is split fifty-fifty. 50% of the content is based on organizational Outcomes and consistent across cohorts inside the same company, and 50% is fully customized by the cohort when the members pick their focus topics.

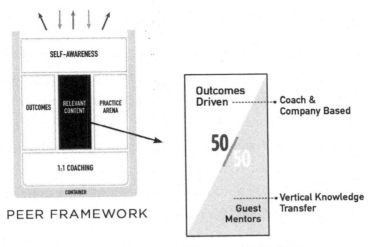

PEER FRAMEWORK

RELEVANT CONTENT

Once the Guest Mentors are chosen, the coach must prepare the Guest Mentors ahead of time (ideally in pairs based on content area). In reviewing the questions generated by the cohort, the Guest Mentor will discover more about the individual Outcomes the cohort members want to learn and achieve. You can manage their expectations that they are to serve in the role of Guest Mentor and not *Guest Presenter*. The goal is for members to hear their stories and best practices. We do not want a PowerPoint presentation about what negotiation should be, but stories of how the Guest Mentors did this well and when they didn't. These stories are more relevant to the company culture. Members want to hear stories of how other mid-career leaders successfully negotiated with them (or not so much). This is the heart of the vertical knowledge transfer.

The Guest Mentors are also steeped in the company culture and context. Instead of bringing in some outside academic or expert on negotiation, introducing relevant negotiation experiences from our company's leaders offers a huge value. The latter is an example of traditional training—PEER coaching layers in the application and the experience around the content and amps up the power exponentially.

For the full 9-month EDGE experience, we facilitate a total of three Guest Mentor sessions, all during the Midpoint session. But these are not formal presentations. They don't deliver worksheets and PowerPoints. It is a facilitated dialogue where the cohort learns from Guest Mentors as they share stories, knowledge, advice, and experiences.

It is important that Guest Mentors are a little farther up the Career Growth Mountain than the cohort members. Their perspective is invaluable and might help members navigate areas of the career labyrinth that look like dead ends. So we bring in those who have been there, done that—leaders who can share best practices so the cohorts themselves can pick what they find most relevant. They co-create the agenda. They co-create the content.

If you are an internal coach, you will see the value Guest Mentors get out of the experience as a way to leverage executive talent and build connections for vertical knowledge transfer inside the organization. For most companies, when they want to engage their executives and leadership development, they assign them to a mentoring program. But this method leaves leaders uninspired.

HORIZONTAL & VERTICAL LEARNING

There are two ways to share and apply best practices around Relevant Content in the PEER Group Coaching Framework— horizontally and vertically. Horizontal happens *between* members of the cohort. Horizontal learning has an inherent limitation. The same peers that bring content to life together also have a significant knowledge restriction: they don't know what they don't know. As a result, they can only share so much. That's why one of the most critical elements of the PEER Framework is vertical knowledge transfer via the Guest Mentors.

> *"One of the most critical elements of the PEER Framework is vertical knowledge transfer via the Guest Mentors."*

One thing I learned quickly is that ninety minutes is a long time for one person to answer questions from a group. Two Guest Mentors is better to keep everyone energized, break up the flow, offer better diversity of experience, and help cover the desired Outcomes. Not only do Guest Mentors impact a lot of people in a relatively short period of time, they also create intentional space for cohort members to expand their actionable networks. In addition, they grow their own executive network by meeting with and engaging a peer of their own, another leader passionate about the same topic. Cohort members gain applicable knowledge from them while the Mentors gain perspective and insights from cohort members and other Guest Mentors. Win. Win. Win.

But it's also important for the Guest Mentors to stay plugged in. For example, Stephanie Doliveira has been a Guest Mentor for me on many occasions and was the executive sponsor for bringing the PEER framework in house at Sheetz. Stephanie leads from the heart with vulnerability.

"Without realizing it, most people naturally limit what they think is possible and what they are capable of achieving. When those barriers are removed, the limits are endless."

In the past, Stephanie had been a Guest Mentor for our open-enrollment group coaching experience at the Pittsburgh Technology Council targeting high-potential women in technology across companies and industries. She arrived at the cohort as the CHRO of Sheetz, but within the first ten minutes, she had authentically shown every woman there that she was just like them. Because she leads Belly-first, Stephanie is always "ALL IN." She embodied the essence of what a good Guest Mentor does—she wanted to galvanize the women to become ambassadors and advocates for one another. She herself became accessible to them by showing her vulnerability first so they could follow her lead.

THE 1:1 CAREER INTERVIEWS

As you read in previous chapters, the 1:1 Career Interviews can have a powerful impact, and their transformative capability has the potential to shift perspectives and break down barriers to success. Why? Without realizing it, most people naturally limit what they think is possible and what they are capable of achieving. When those barriers are removed, the limits are endless.

1:1 Career Interviews create space for each cohort member to find a senior leader to connect with, learn from, and perhaps even begin to cultivate a relationship with them as a potential mentor and sponsor. Participants choose any leader from inside or outside the company, someone with whom they want to build credibility and visibility. They interview them for the purpose of learning from the leader and share what was learned with the entire cohort. In this way, everybody gets the experience of being inspired from this leader and their career journey.

Then, when any cohort members either reach out to or encounter this leader in the future, they can have an authentic conversation about what was learned and start building their own relationship. The result? Everybody receives insights from these 1:1 Career Interviews about leaders they would otherwise never have known.

In short, after Relevant Content brings such diverse knowledge transfer, your cohort members are now ready to practice, practice, practice. In the following chapter, I'll show you the value of maintaining an intentional space, or Practice Arena, in which they can work.

IGNITE: BEST PRACTICES

✓ Relevant Content only takes up about 10% of the experience, but that 10% is critical.

✓ The organizational Outcomes should drive around 85% of the content. After all, it is the organization that's paying for the experience.

✓ Create the space for vertical knowledge transfer. About 50% of Relevant Content is content that you, the coach, bring based on research and data. Use a maximum of three total competencies, one of which is coaching related.

✓ The other 50% of the Relevant Content comes from bringing in Guest Mentors to share experiences and best practices around content that is co-created by the cohort.

✓ Introduce diversity of thought and experiences through Guest Mentors in a thoughtful way that amplifies your organizational Outcomes.

✓ While the first part of the Relevant Content is driven by the organizational Outcomes, the second part must be co-created by the peer group. I recommend offering a menu of topics from which the cohort can pick.

✓ It is important that Guest Mentors are a little farther up the Career Growth Mountain than the cohort members. Their perspective is invaluable and might help members navigate areas of the career labyrinth that look like dead ends.

✓ There are two ways to share and apply best practices around Relevant Content in the PEER Group Coaching Framework—horizontally and vertically.

- Horizontal knowledge transfer happens *between* members of the cohort.
- Vertical knowledge transfer happens via the Guest Mentors.

✓ 1:1 Career Interviews create space for each cohort member to find a senior leader to connect with to learn from and perhaps even cultivate a relationship with as a potential mentor and sponsor.

THOUGHT SPARKS

1. *What really resonated for you around the concept of Relevant Content? Why does this feel important to you right now?*

2. *What content could you curate that would be relevant to your audience? What research do you have on it? Why are you passionate about it?*

3. *How often do your clients or coachees have input into content selection?*

4. *If you were going to create a Guest Mentor Topic Menu, what topics would you choose?*

5. *Do you have a diverse pool of executives you could pull from when looking for Guest Mentors? What can you do to increase these connections?*

6. *How does your current coaching program help develop both horizontal and vertical knowledge transfer within an organization? What works well? What doesn't?*

Tips for Concentrated Experiences

While the Guest Mentor concept works well in the 2-day Jumpstart group coaching experience, there simply isn't enough time to weave it into a shorter approach in a thoughtful way. The value of a peer group experience is always first and foremost the peer group itself. If you take 50% of the time in a 1 or 2 hour experience to focus on the Guest Mentor (instead of bonding and connecting them together), all you get is, at worst, a keynote address or, at best, a fireside chat. While that has value, it will not help you achieve your Outcomes of peer connection and group coaching with your clients.

For a 1-hour Coaching Circle, I survey the audience ahead of time, asking where they are stuck both personally and professionally and invite them to define what success looks like. I use the data to find trends, then adjust the best practices content for the session. Next, I tee up four possible topics and ask which topics feel most relevant to them in the moment to work through. In this way, you can quickly layer in co-creating in a powerful way. We must allow our cohort members in all sessions to embody choice because choice is at the heart of all group coaching.

Then I share best practices around the topics they chose and set them up to discuss in small groups. Finally, I drop them into a breakout to connect with an accountability partner to create their first step in change. They leave the session with a peer who will hold them accountable to take that new, first step in whatever challenge they want to address.

In a 2-hour Coaching Circle, I recommend you as the coach share best practices around the content that serves the organizational Outcomes of your client. In fact, I often frame these sessions by saying that the best practices I am sharing are not mine, but learned from the thousands of leaders I've had the privilege of learning from. In this way, you also incorporate the voices of peers who could not join the group and keep yourself (as always) from being center stage. If you do not frame it in this way, it can easily look like the spotlight is on you in a shorter session.

But, in a 2-day Jumpstart experience, there's enough time to incorporate a full Guest Mentor session and teach basic group coaching skills. I layer in Relevant Content that meets the organizational Outcomes, some content nuggets to learn and discuss, then go through the Career Growth Mountain concepts of coaching, mentoring, and advocacy.

For example, I may give twenty minutes of relevant content nuggets to a high-potential group, then immediately get them into small breakout groups to talk about it. *How did it resonate? What didn't? Why? How do you see this play out here in our company? What is the cost?* They learn together and from one another, but it is definitely not a stale PowerPoint presentation that screams, *This is the content!*

They move from group to group every twenty minutes or so. As a result, they stay plugged in because they know the content will be relevant to the conversations taking place as they co-create it. And that's it.

THE PRACTICE ARENA

"Fitting in is about assessing a situation and becoming who you need to be to be accepted. Belonging, on the other hand, doesn't require us to change who we are; it requires us to be who we are."

— DR. BRENÉ BROWN

When I talk about the Practice Arena, I'm talking about creating an intentional developmental space to begin to apply the new skills learned in the PEER Group Coaching experience. Each person gets the opportunity to become both the student and the teacher, the coach and the coachee. Everyone becomes a contributor to the learning and growth of others in the group. It's where we all practice giving and receiving. It is a space of action, an opportunity to give permission both to be contributed to and be a contributor.

It is a Practice Arena where cohort members can leverage all their new tools and apply them in a safe space. However, there needs to be some kind of intentional vehicle through which they can do that. And this is yet another part where the peer group truly co-creates the work.

It all starts with Self-Awareness. To engage in this space, people have to think first about what they are proud of, what they want to celebrate, and also be able to clearly identify their struggles. They need to have a purposeful space of vulnerability and trust, a place where they can avoid trying to recreate the wheel and solve problems on their own.

The honest truth is, I have personally grown and transformed right alongside each and every cohort I have ever coached. This is because each time we launch a new cohort, I, too, set my own individual Outcome and model vulnerability by sharing my journey as we move through the Relevant Content experiences.

As coaches, we typically go into this field because *we* love growth. We love to challenge ourselves, and ultimately we are learners at heart. I find my own development is exponentially heightened by doing PEER Group Coaching work. It is invaluable to me. I wouldn't have written this book, for example, without sharing my journey of conceiving of it and the challenges I've faced along the way with my 2022 cohorts.

The world is missing this intentional developmental space now more than ever. Western culture has convinced society that everyone should be self-sufficient, that it is somehow a weakness to need each other. And it often makes us feel inadequate when we don't know what to do next. But that is not the way humans are wired. In fact, this cultural shift is a recent phenomenon. People have lived for centuries in villages and tribes—in community. We've leaned on one another when needed and celebrated the successes that a single person may overlook or not

> "Western culture has convinced society that everyone should be self-sufficient, that it is somehow a weakness to need each other."

honor in the same way your community does. The PEER Group Coaching Framework is based on these ancient principles, so of course people get excited when they, maybe for the first time in their adult lives, feel like they found a genuine community of peers.

Every time someone shares a success, they contribute to those around them. Unfortunately, society has also conditioned us to think that sharing a success is boasting, but it actually opens the door of contribution to other people and helps them achieve their Outcomes and goals. I must confess that I'm a really good "giver." I love to give to people. Giving makes me feel confident and competent. I just feel good when I can give to others. However, that isn't the case at all for my natural ability to receive. Metaphorically, my "giving arm" is over-developed like Popeye's, but my "receiving arm" is underdeveloped, like Olive

Oyl's. It's just not exercised enough to have built much muscle. Candidly, receiving makes me feel inadequate, like I'm not good enough. As a result, I often *over* give to compensate.

Using PEER-centered group coaching and this idea of creating intentional space for sharing creates a purposeful balance of giving *and* receiving. A cohort member can't share a challenge unless they also share a success and vice versa. Instead of *either/or*, the Practice Arena is the space of *both/and*.

In my experience in PEER groups, women struggle most with sharing successes. As a coach, I firmly but gently encourage cohort members to think about something they're proud of. More often than not, people are usually only willing to share a success if it is a *raging* success. But in reality, even small successes are valid and important. It could be that I gave myself permission to take a nap this past weekend and not be productive. Or that I made time for a date night out on the deck with Kevin and my favorite beverage.

"Everybody struggles to ask for help."

Conversely, I've seen many men struggle with admitting challenges. American men typically have less hesitation sharing successes, but often struggle to admit they struggle. However, across the gender, age, race and ethnicity spectrums, everybody struggles with asking for help. Once a person chooses to practice vulnerability and express a challenge in our PEER Framework, they receive the gift of a wealth of best practice ideas from the cohort to explore.

Sharing successes is a gift. One cohort member's success this month could easily be someone else's challenge two months from now. And when that challenge comes, that person knows exactly who in their network has advice and best practices to offer—the network is ignited. And every time someone shares a success or a challenge, they also exercise their muscle of being their own advocate and living their personal brand. Every time they open up and practice vulnerability, it makes being vulnerable the next time that much easier. But just as important as the sharing is the generous response cohort members give in return.

As I said earlier, I often remind the group that the very best response to anything that is shared in the PEER Group Coaching experience is simply, "Thank you." This response eliminates judgment (or comparison) and focuses on acknowledgment and acceptance. Every time a perceived judgment (outside or inside the person's own head) holds someone back from sharing, it discourages others from sharing themselves. It's all part of maintaining and amplifying the Container that has been built.

This is the kind of detail that matters a lot. It's where the rubber meets the road. In group coaching, always remember that it's *their* struggles and *their* solutions. They are here to learn from their peers in this space by both giving and receiving. We are not hired as consultants to "fix" anyone. Even if they ask us to.

SHARING: THE HEART OF INTENTIONAL SPACE

Heather Bell participated in the 9-month EDGE experience, but when she walked into the Launch session, she felt like she wasn't accomplished enough to be there. She was feeling some serious imposter syndrome. She had just begun a new management role, and here she was, surrounded by peers who seemed so accomplished. The truth is she felt intimidated. However, as the cohort members got to know each other, Heather discovered a secret—everyone else felt the same way!

Heather's personal experience had cast a shadow over her perceptions and created a sense of self-doubt. You see, Heather is a domestic abuse survivor. She was married young to her highschool sweetheart who emotionally and verbally abused Heather for twelve years. Between gaslighting and the inability to stand up for herself at the time, she eventually felt as though she deserved the bad things that happened to her.

Throughout that time, her self-confidence was stripped from her, leaving behind a woman who felt incapable, unqualified, and unworthy. Even after the relationship ended, Heather always had a negative story playing inside her head. During the Launch session, that script was still playing, telling her horrible things about herself.

In the past, Heather had avoided sharing her story. She felt shame about calling herself a domestic abuse survivor because her wounds were not visible. She also worried it might take away from women who "had it worse." However, in the safety of the Practice Arena we created, Heather wanted to be truthful about her past. She thought if she did not share her story, it would not be fair to herself nor the other women in the cohort who wanted to know her. The environment of trust within the intentional space inspired and propelled Heather towards practicing courage. And with that courage came the gifts of vulnerability and forgiveness. She knew she needed to bring her whole self to the conversation to maximize the PEER group opportunity that was in front of her.

Exercising that sharing muscle is exactly what Heather Bell did. At first, because of her lack of confidence, Heather made herself very small. Even as she read her "I Am From" story to the other cohort members, she stayed completely focused on the piece of paper in front of her and tried not to make eye contact. She just wanted to get through it.

But when she looked up after sharing, she saw that one of her fellow cohort sisters had tears streaming down her face. The woman let her know that she had gone through a similar situation. Other women nodded that they could also relate. Heather realized there were other women for whom she had opened a door of understanding, all by sharing her story.

For the first time ever, Heather felt safe to share her truth with a room full of people, her cohort sisters. She no longer saw work colleagues. She saw friends. In that moment, Heather felt humble, supported, and seen. When she got to see herself through her sisters' eyes, it had a transformative effect on her. It felt good to share something so big with others and not be judged.

> "She no longer saw work colleagues. She saw friends."

Over the course of the PEER Group Coaching experience, the women who had once intimidated Heather became her most trusted confidants with whom she still shares professional challenges and consults when she needs different perspectives she can trust. Her sharing (and their receiving) made them all stronger and more confident to bring their best to the world every day because of this intentional space.

> In my PEER experience, the details of every person's story were different (they involved children, parents, marriages, finances, co-workers, jobs, etc.) but evoked a common realization from us all. Everyone is in some stage of processing, solution-ing, overcoming, or wrestling with our own demons and challenges that life throws at us. Learning this was eye-opening and lent us all strength. For me, it brought a camaraderie and honest connection that serves as additional scaffolding to my foundation. It made me realize helping to move the needle of success for others is the secret to contributing to my own.
>
> **—Deb Ing,**
> *Scrum master, PNC Bank*

Another way to curate this Practice Arena is through monthly Triad sessions where the peers practice coaching one another. One participant asks a thought-provoking question such as, "What do you want to focus on for coaching today?" Then the next participant thinks about the question and practices vulnerability by sharing a current personal or professional challenge. Another question that might be asked is, "How does that tie to your Outcome for this year's experience?" And so on.

Every time they enter into the Triad Coaching Practice Arena, each coachee identifies their next steps and what they want to do differently. The third person in each Triad plays the role of the Observer (more on this in the next chapter) and provides timely feedback to the coach. Everyone feels their challenge is individual, but they soon discover that they are not alone in their struggles. In addition to coaching within the Triad, they also need a powerful best-practice-sharing vehicle for more horizontal knowledge transfer to take place—the Mastermind.

THE MASTERMIND AT WORK

In my experience, the Mastermind is the most elegant and simple peer-learning vehicle. I did not invent the Mastermind, of course. In fact, Benjamin Franklin is often credited for having done so, but I have found it to be the best vehicle to bring to life a dynamic intentional developmental space for sharing and growth.

I learned about the Mastermind from a fellow coach, a mentor, and dear friend of mine, Mary Ann Fatheddin, in my very first cohort, the working mothers group. The Mastermind was used in large companies like General Electric where she worked in Talent Development, and she introduced me to it. Because Mary Ann had a daughter who was older than my son, I often went to her for parenting advice. She suggested it would be great to leverage it to get input from more seasoned mothers as a framework for our monthly meetings.

You may recall that I hinted at this process earlier. At the heart of the Mastermind, each person does three things: share a Success, share a Challenge, and make a Request for Support. The beautiful thing about this sequence is the requirement that cohort members can't share a Challenge until they share a Success first. Successes may be tied to their Outcomes or to other challenges in their personal or professional life. For some people like me, sharing their successes is hard. For some, it is more difficult to share real, vulnerable Challenges. For others, asking for help feels uncomfortable and new. Within the Mastermind, everyone can find their learning edge.

"Wrapping words around what doesn't feel good to me in my work or home life moves me to act."

Remember that PEER Group Coaching is especially powerful because language is generative—speaking it aloud takes the idea out of one person's mind and puts it out into the world. Wrapping words around what doesn't feel good to me in my work or home life moves me to act. The intentional developmental space allows everyone to stop avoiding (well, whatever they are avoiding right now) and purposefully step into the Practice Arena where they can show courage. When they speak a Challenge out loud and become open to other perspectives, they will be more apt to actually do something about it. Plus, when we verbalize both Successes and Challenges, it helps us understand that we don't have to be perfect, and, just as importantly, it opens us to receiving help from others.

Because all of our six PEER Group Coaching Elements are intrinsically tied to one another in the PEER Group Coaching Framework, a person's Success is often be tied to their application of Relevant Content. At this stage of the experience, we want to help our cohort members avoid getting stuck trying to be the perfect coach, because this aspect of the Framework is *not* about coaching, but creating the space for each person to receive and contribute feedback, advice, and best practices. The Practice Arena creates patterns for everyone to follow up on those Requests for Support later—so everyone has the opportunity to contribute.

"That's the power of the peer group—when successes happen and are shared, everyone benefits. The contributors that help give advice and suggestions also become receivers."

Advice and connections happen during the monthly Mastermind activity of course, but the learning doesn't stop there. Some of the most powerful connections and conversations occur over the course of the following month after the Mastermind meets. I often say the PEER magic is in the "in-between" sessions—where resources are located and innovations are leveraged. These are connections only companions on this shared journey could offer. That's the power of the peer group—when successes happen and are shared, everyone benefits. The contributors that help give advice and suggestions also become receivers. Each leans more into vulnerability as they give themselves permission to speak their Belly truth and to allow themselves to be seen. And with every Request for Support, every new idea generated is a fresh chance to live bravely. The successes multiply as everyone gets uplifted. By the way, as a coach, I rarely offer advice during the Request for Support section, because it's not about us. It's always about them learning from one another; it's *their* vehicle for knowledge transfer.

We leverage the Mastermind in every one of our PEER Group Coaching experiences—whether 2 hours, 2 days, or 9 months. The best practices in this chapter around executing this developmental vehicle apply to them all. The only difference is that in longer experiences, it is consistently utilized in every single monthly session.

"There is equal value in sharing and in holding space for others to share."

In each instance, regardless of whether the PEER Group Coaching experience is in-person or virtual, we always divide into groups of around six people. Every cohort member in each group has six minutes to share. In less than a 40-minute time period, everyone gets the opportunity to both share and contribute. The result? Engagement and innovation spikes! While I have tried doing this in larger groupings, I've found that if the size is too large, our more introverted folks can feel hesitant to share. A small group feels more intimate and creates stronger connections in a powerful way. I feel the same way about the actual time allotted per person. Any more than six minutes and our more extroverted folks start to get imaginative and focus more on their story and less on creating space to efficiently find a resolution. Six minutes is enough to satisfy extroverts, yet not too much to overwhelm our introverts. As always, each cohort member is given the choice to share or not share in each session. Of course, as we discussed earlier, there is equal value in sharing and in holding space for others to share.

When teeing up a session using the Mastermind as a vehicle in the Practice Arena, begin by explaining the activity and expectations. When it is the first time explaining the process, I always recommend that you use this opportunity to again model vulnerability and share a personal Challenge. Share what is truly cooking for you that month, week, or day. Remember, if you stay at the professional level, most participants will as well. By being the first to go personal, you will be surprised by how many follow. As I shared earlier, I usually try to select a Challenge that has to do with a family member or with showing myself self-compassion around a current challenge I am facing. Depending on what is authentically going on for me at the time, it is typically in relation to a sibling, in-law, husband, or my teenage son.

As with every activity in our PEER Group Coaching Framework, I strongly encourage you to manage their time for them. This keeps the knowledge transfer flowing, and ensures everyone has adequate space to share. Always create the space for choice by reminding them there is enough time for everyone in their group to share a Success, Challenge, and Request for Support. Because the element of choice is so integral to our experience, it is always an option to skip sharing that day if they choose. (I tell them that I promise there will always be someone in their group who will happily use up their available time!) In a virtual setting, I send cohort members broadcast messages in their breakouts to alert them when to move on to the next person. After the session with the Mastermind, cohort members now each have five new accountability partners to regularly connect with.

When you bring them back to debrief after the Mastermind breakout, always start by slowly warming the large group: "Who heard a Success that inspired them?" Ask for raised hands or, in a virtual setting, emojis. Then, invite them to practice being big and bold and share a Success they are personally proud of. This creates the space to extend the Practice Arena to the bigger environment. Then go right into asking who has a Request for Support they want to share to the larger group. Now, it is possible to leverage the "hive mind" at large and create an intentional space for the larger group to contribute to the best practice sharing and to exponentially increase the knowledge transfer.

DIVERSITY IN THE GROUPS

What makes the Practice Arena especially powerful is the inclusion that exists within the peer group. If everyone is the same age with the same experiences, the group will miss out on the value of diverse contributions. However, the diverse cohort should ideally always be in a similar developmental space on the Growth Mountain.

As the group coach, it is important to be thoughtful about experience areas within the company to ensure a good mix. For example, it may be a mix of people from out in the field and from the HQ offices, or between business units, regions, countries, departments, and focus areas. We also need diversity across race and ethnicity, sexual orientation, and gender, to name a few. Without diversity, a lot of important perspectives and ideas get missed.

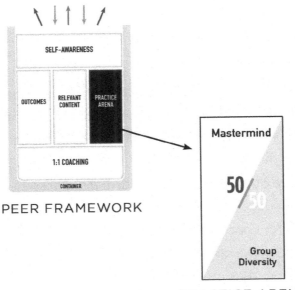

PEER FRAMEWORK

PRACTICE ARENA

For example, as a White facilitator and group coach, I can bring my learning about trying to be actively anti-racist and my experiences of my own White fragility, but I certainly don't have firsthand experience of what it means to be a Black woman in corporate America right now. Acknowledging that, I can intentionally create the space to elevate the voices of the women of color in the cohort and ensure that Guest Mentors also purposefully represent people who do not look like me. I can be thoughtful about layering Relevant Content that is from Black authors, articles about what it means to be Asian American right now, and so forth. The success of the PEER Group Coaching experience is incredibly dependent on layering in equity and focusing on inclusion.

> Previous leadership cohorts have felt very competitive, as if we were all competing for the same jobs, with little to no support. What my PEER experience gave me was a group of women who genuinely want to see other women succeed, and support them in that success. The group of women are chosen so well and each of us has so much to offer others. The diverse range of experience, age, careers, and backgrounds is a great reminder that while we tend to live in our own little bubbles, there is so much more to experience in the world.
>
> **—Taryn Malavite,**
> *Senior Manager IT Business Solutions, Duquesne Light Co.*

So how many minority cohort members do you need in the group to ensure they have the confidence to be vulnerable and share so all may learn? In my experience, three or more people in a minority group gives power (less than that and experience has likely shown them that it is often not safe to speak at the Belly level), but you have magic when you have at least 20% of your total group enrollment. When that happens, it creates a beautiful tapestry of rich dialogue within a peer group.

RECOMMENDED COHORT DIVERSITY

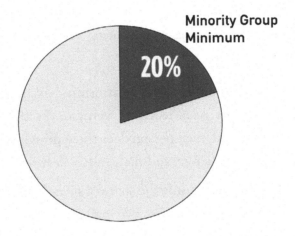

Masterminds and Coaching Triad groups are integral to the Practice Arena by creating a space to share best practices and get the most of the PEER Group Coaching experience. In the next chapter, I'll discuss how 1:1 Coaching amplifies this accountability and support and helps cohort members dive deeper to access greater levels of growth and success.

IGNITE: BEST PRACTICES

✓ The world is missing a Practice Arena now more than ever, an intentional space for sharing vulnerable challenges and receiving best practices.

✓ In my experience, the Mastermind is the most elegant and simple peer-learning vehicle. At the heart of the Mastermind, each person does three things: share a Success, share a Challenge, and make a Request for Support.

- Every time someone shares a success, they contribute to those around them. We invite them to redefine success sharing—it is not bragging. Your Success this month could be someone else's Challenge next month. For some, sharing successes is hard. For others, expressing vulnerability around a current personal or professional challenge is difficult. For still others, the hard part is asking for help. Everyone can find their learning edge in the Practice Arena.

- A cohort member can't share a Challenge unless they also share a Success, and vice versa. Instead of *either/or*, the Practice Arena is the space of *both/and*.

- With each Request for Support, every new idea generated is a fresh chance to live bravely. The successes multiply as everyone gets uplifted.

- Regardless of whether it is in-person or virtual, divide people into groups of around six. Each cohort member in each group has six minutes to share. Within a thirty-minute time period, each member gets the opportunity to both share and contribute.

- As with every activity in our PEER Group Coaching Framework, I strongly encourage you to manage their time for them.

✓ Powerful connections and conversations can occur in the month following the Mastermind and Coaching Triad time. The magic is in the "in-between" sessions—where resources are located and innovations are leveraged.

✓ Be thoughtful about ensuring diversity and equity within the group. Without diversity, a lot of important perspectives and ideas get missed. In addition, this inclusion creates a beautiful tapestry of rich dialogue within a peer group.

THOUGHT SPARKS

1. *What really resonates with you around this new concept of a Practice Arena? Where could you apply it? How?*

2. *What is a recent personal or professional success you are proud of?*

3. *What is hard for you around sharing your successes? Why do you think that is?*

4. *What is a challenge you can see for yourself in incorporating PEER Group Coaching into your practice?*

5. *If you could make any Request for Support from a more experienced PEER Group Coach, what would it be?*

6. *Do you see differences across the gender spectrum, race, culture, or ethnicity show up in your clients in either celebrating success or sharing challenges? How?*

1:1 COACHING

*"The master has failed more times
than the beginner has tried."*

— STEPHEN MCCRANIE

Connie Eaton has always been a logical person. Before taking part in her open-enrollment PEER experience, she worried it would be a little "fluffier" than she prefered. She knew she wanted to leave her company. She had gone from IT Consultant, to Manager, to Associate Director, to Director and felt she had reached the end of her growth potential there. Although successful, she felt like she was living someone else's dream.

So as she began her group coaching experience, Connie just wanted to figure out how to meet people and make contacts in the Pittsburgh area to find opportunities and see what her next move would be. She found that, but also something much more valuable: the confidence, insights, and understanding needed to help her make the next move in a powerful and intentional way. She didn't realize there were other possibilities to own her career (and her life), and up until that point in her life had never really asked herself what she wanted.

Connie is not alone. In fact, a lot of people take whatever role they can get when first starting out. But after fifteen or twenty years, they find they have invested time and effort into something that really isn't what they wanted. Others find their desires and interests evolved but are still living on autopilot, following an outdated flight plan. They fail to realize the possibility that they could achieve something different. Something more meaningful. More *them*.

When I talked about 1:1 Coaching earlier, I unpacked how coaching, mentoring, and advocacy work. However, the best way to understand what I mean by 1:1 Coaching in the PEER Framework is to first understand what it is not.

Coaching is about being a companion. It is nothing more than a critical thinking process by which we help someone else solve their own challenges. And as each of us reading this book knows, coaching transforms lives.

As I stated earlier in the book, coaching is *not* therapy. Therapy is about looking back at where you have been and making sense of how the past affects the choices you are making right now and the limitations that you may be putting on yourself. Coaching is a conversation between two people, one of whom companions the other to help look forward and see where they want most to go next.

In other words, if therapy is standing where I am and looking back, coaching is about standing where I am and looking forward to discovering where I want to go. It's about reflection and strategic choices. *How am I getting in my own way? What do I want to change? What could I do differently?* (Ideally a 1:1 Coach is certified by accredited organizations such as the International Coaching Federation (ICF), where coaches go through a certification process to train and have continuing education requirements to maintain.)

> "If therapy is standing where I am and looking back, coaching is about standing where I am and looking forward to discovering where I want to go."

1:1 Coaching is *not* consulting. It is not about someone telling someone else what to do. Coaching is about asking engaging questions and being a thinking partner. Imagine we are walking through the woods together. Your goal is to get to the waterfall at the southern face of the Growth Mountain. As a coach, I don't grab your arm and pull you to the waterfall. I don't get behind you and push you, steer you to the left or right, or urge you to walk faster. I simply walk beside you.

If you want to stop and have lunch by the creek with the willow trees, we stop and have lunch, and I get curious, asking you questions. *Why did you pick here? What do you like about the creek? What are you hungry for?* Then I may ask, *How do you know when you are ready to get up and head over? Do you want to stay here a little bit longer?* Then perhaps before we reach the waterfall, you change your mind. You want to investigate a new path. And that's fine with me, because 1:1 Coaching is never about the coach.

Great 1:1 Coaching is about companioning you as the coachee in your evolution, recognizing your ideal outcome, checking in regularly, and always being a good accountability partner. The role of a coach is to first and foremost call you to be your best self. The term I learned in my coaching school at Newfield Network is *gentle irreverence.* 1:1 Coaching is about asking tough questions and honoring the fact that you are a whole and healthy individual and know the best ways to solve your challenges. Your solutions are already there inside of you. A good coach simply helps you achieve that potential.

> "The role of a coach is to first and foremost call you to be your best self."

For me, 1:1 Coaching is the backbone of the whole PEER framework. It's what makes group coaching just that: *coaching,* not training or group facilitation. The only way cohort members in a peer group can coach and support one another is to learn how to become coaches themselves. At the heart of group coaching are cohort members who learn how to coach, practice coaching each other both during and between the group sessions, and then also put that skill into practicing it in their personal and professional lives. They become the connecting parts and pieces for the entire process. If we as coaches don't teach *them* how to coach, the PEER model becomes just one more training program. This is why the Relevant Content must always include the competency of Coaching.

In training, the instructor delivers the content while the person being trained learns the content and, hopefully, applies it. But in group coaching, the coach is not the focal point. The peer group is.

DIVING DEEPER

Our challenge in coaching is figuring out how to create the space for a person to generate their own ideas. Most of us are so busy *doing* all the time that we rarely have the time to critically think through our challenges. That's one of the greatest gifts of 1:1 Coaching. I can't tell you how many people come into Office Hours with me (more on that later) and tell me they've been looking forward to it for weeks. For them, it's a space to let whatever is going to come out come out. They don't feel like they have to have all the right answers. They can simply sit and reflect about their challenge. They can ideate without fear of judgment.

That sacred space is a gift that can be transformative, as we coaches know and have seen play out time and again in our own personal and professional lives. At the end of the day during the second month of her EDGE experience, Tina (not her real name) had not said a word in the large group setting. I had gone through an entire full day of teaching coaching skills and creating space in the Practice Arena. While everybody else worked on an activity , she simply sat in the back of the room, big tears rolling down her face. At that time, Tina was probably nearly a hundred pounds overweight and intentionally nondescript in appearance. She later shared with me that she did everything in her power to fade into the background of wherever she found herself. That day, she was hiding quietly in the back of the room. Tina had staged her briefcases and bags on either side of her, almost as if she was making sure to keep her walls up and boundaries firm.

"As group coaches, it is a necessary skill to hold the space for the room (virtual or in-person) while simultaneously connecting to each individual."

As group coaches, it is a necessary skill to hold the space for the room (virtual or in-person) while simultaneously connecting to each individual. The flames of both are equal and necessary. I went over to her quietly while everybody else was working in groups and knelt down beside her so our faces were at equal levels (because coaches are always equals). I did not ask her what was wrong. Instead I let her know she didn't need to stay in the room, that she had full permission to take care of herself. I also asked her how I could help. Her tears spilled over the walls and became a flowing torrent.

I stayed beside her while she took a breath. "I'm going to step outside," she said. "I'm going to collect myself. But can I talk with you 1:1 after the session ends?" Later that afternoon, when everyone else headed back to their hotel rooms to prepare for dinner, Tina began to open up to me. Everything she had been struggling with just poured out of her in a tangled wave of emotion: how unhappy she was in her job and in her marriage. She had three kids. Her teenage daughter was getting into all kinds of trouble. Her husband was a truck driver and gone for days at a time. She was working as a woman in a male-dominated transportation industry. She shared that she had been with the company for more than twenty years and had never experienced the depth of what she was feeling in the PEER group setting. She had simply become overwhelmed by everything she had finally allowed herself to *feel* for the first time. So I stayed beside her and dropped into some 1:1 Coaching that felt organic and powerful for the both of us.

That breakthrough of naming her feelings—and her dissatisfaction in her life—was the beginning of a transformation in Tina. The next day, I watched her move from table to table and begin to find her voice in the room. She signed up for Office Hours with me the next month and made regular appointments. For seven of the nine months of the experience, she engaged in 1:1 Coaching with me. If the spots were full for the month, she put herself on the waitlist. She even asked everybody in the group (one month it was her actual Request for Support in the Mastermind) to let her know if they ended up not using their Office Hours spot.

By the end of the experience, not only did Tina share her story of transformation to the executives of her company at Continuation, but she had lost nearly sixty pounds! She reinvented herself and called herself "Tina 2.0." After twenty years in Operations, she applied for a promotion in Learning and

Development where they were creating a brand-new role that no one had ever been in before. She told them in the interview, "I have fallen in love with coaching. Put me in! I not only will help you create this new role, but I'll also help the company shape the best practices in how we can replicate it across North America." And she did.

In the years to follow, Tina became a Certified Health Coach. Tina is also now an Ironman triathlete. She won state and national competitions. She ended up divorcing her husband and now has an amazing grandson in her life. All three of her daughters are also thriving.

Tina would proudly tell you today, nearly ten years later, all of the positive improvements were seeded because of PEER Group Coaching. By no means am I saying it was because of me. Just the opposite. It was Tina. Tina was the one who acknowledged in that second month session of EDGE that she was ready to change. She didn't know how this brand-new concept of coaching was going to help her, but she knew it was time to stop hiding, and she felt peace that she didn't have to figure it all out on her own. Was it all at once? Did she decide to tackle everything that was not going well in her life all at the same time? No. She started with the first (not so small step) of showing herself compassion and prioritizing taking care of herself.

She went "ALL IN" in the PEER coaching within her Triads, bringing her juiciest challenges to be coached. She channeled her empathy and experience into becoming a stellar coach herself for her peers. She gave herself permission to go deeper and harder, to get into the heavier stuff and become more vulnerable. She took risks. She owned the fact that she was deeply unhappy, and perhaps for the first time in her adult life, felt empowered that she could do something about it.

This was a woman who did not like the way she looked, the way she felt, her level of energy, the way she was parenting, the state of her marriage, and the way she was showing up at work. She changed it all with the help of coaching. Tina ignited.

EMPOWERING CHANGE

To have a true PEER group coaching experience you must first and foremost teach all participants how to become coaches. After creating the Container, 1:1 Coaching is foundational to our PEER Framework, which is why it spans the entire foundation of the Framework. Coaching is like the fiber optic lines that connect everything together while sharing the lights of each cohort member. I know there are people out there who define group coaching as putting a person in the front of the room to "coach" an entire group, but in my experience of doing this work over the last fifteen years, that is neither efficient nor effective.

In my experience as an L&D professional, training is typically taking off-the-shelf content and hammering out a bunch of skills via a slide deck and a binder of materials for people to learn to memorize and hopefully apply. Facilitation is moving folks through discussions along an agenda for people to achieve a shared group Outcome. The coaching piece is very different. Coaching is an equal power, dynamic relationship where both people come to the table with a vested interest in the Outcome *of the coachee.* As a coach, we know our job is really to help people figure out their own possibilities, their own solutions, and to have their own "aha!" moments through asking purposeful, insightful, meaningful questions. Through the PEER Group Coaching Framework, we get to open the door for others to fall in love with coaching, just like we did.

"Coaching is about supporting someone in their Self-Awareness as they uncover the real issues behind their challenges."

That's why it is important for us first to educate our cohort members on what 1:1 Coaching is not. It's not training. Nor is it facilitation. And it's definitely not about giving advice nor solving problems for the coachee. Coaching is about supporting someone in their Self-Awareness as they uncover the real issues behind their challenges. Too often in coaching the novice coach thinks the person has a problem to be fixed. Their over-used and over-developed problem solving or "giving muscles" come out, the same ones they are rewarded for using every day in their jobs. But as experienced coaches know all too well, most coachees often first bring something to the table that is not the real core issue. The real issue is underneath the story. Coaching is asking the right questions to discover possibilities and openings that had not been able to be seen before.

Let me illustrate what I mean. As an executive, integral coach, and certified diversity practitioner, Felicia Byrd, PCC, spent the last twenty years as the Head of Diversity and Inclusion Consulting at Wells Fargo. Felicia has a passion for helping people, and her purpose is to encourage people to discover their goals. As a seasoned coach, Felicia understands how important asking insightful and impactful questions can be when helping people think about their journey.

Felicia really thrives on group coaching. She loves bringing people together, not to train them nor provide solutions for them, but to help them create their own possibilities. She believes that group coaching actually helps people understand themselves at all levels: Head, Heart, and Belly.

Felicia was impacted by the authenticity of the PEER Group Coaching Framework and the encouragement for people to be their true, genuine selves: "Throughout my thirty-plus year career, I looked for leaders who were genuine, who seemed to be authentic and real. Humans make mistakes, and it is okay for people to admit they don't know everything and don't have all the answers, especially leaders."

Leveraging someone else's philosophy and approach can be scary and challenging, but Felicia trusted the PEER Group Coaching Framework and began using it herself in her own coaching activities in her private practice. The PEER Framework worked. As she describes it,

"Isn't that the greatest legacy we can have? To make an impact even after we are no longer present."

"When people learn from their peers, it is extremely effective and self-sustaining. It breaks down a lot of barriers for leaders who often think they have to know all the answers, solve all the problems, and be perfect at everything. It provides an opening and an opportunity for leaders to bond with each other and not feel so alone in their leadership."

I love it when other coaches catch the PEER vision and use it in their own domains, because just as we see in our cohorts, when we can teach people the skill of coaching, they ignite each other. By the end of it all, we don't even need to be there anymore, because *guess what?* We won't be there forever. Eventually, our coachees have to create and sustain this capacity on their own. They build a skill beside their peers and practice it in a safe space. Our job as a coach is to create the space for them to try, fail, reflect, engage to try it again, and learn. And isn't that the greatest legacy we can have? To make an impact even after we are no longer present.

I have said it before and will say it again: the PEER group coaching experience is not about us as the coach; it is always about the peer group. As the group coach, about 25% of our role in each and every experience is to set the stage for the development of this coaching capacity, to teach operation leaders, entrepreneurs, sales managers, CEOs, or even parents of transgender kids how to do what we do—how to be coaches. In other words, the challenge is to teach the coaching skill to someone who's not a professional coach.

This marks a big distinction between what passes for group coaching and what PEER Group Coaching looks like when it is being used effectively. As you may have seen, most traditional group coaching frameworks often have one coach for a group of fewer than ten people. But being the only coach for everybody in the group means you are the source of all expertise. The coach is the one doing the work.

TRADITIONAL GROUP COACHING

Conversely, the cohort members in the PEER Framework are always the ones doing the heavy lifting. You teach, then model a skill. Then you step aside and let them practice that skill, supporting them when they do it well and equally when they don't. The Container allows them to use the intentional developmental space as the Practice Arena. To use an old analogy, you aren't gifting everyone a fabulous fish dinner; you are teaching people how to catch and fry their own fish.

The beautiful thing is this: not only do cohort members coach one another, but every time they do so, they build relationships in the Practice Arena, reinforce the Container, embrace vulnerability, increase Self-Awareness, and practice applying Relevant Content. In other words, everything that has been built in the PEER Framework is touched by this coaching practice. Once again, coaching makes the transmission and illumination of everyone's lights possible and amplifies them all in a kaleido-scope of mirrors.

1:1 Coaching is especially important because there is accountability in it as each cohort member serves as a coach to the others. After every Triad Time, the cohort-member coach checks in with the coachee, following up in the way that's most helpful to that person. The goal of any coach is to help someone figure out whatever their first step is with their particular challenge, then ensure they not only take it, but more importantly, reflect and learn from it.

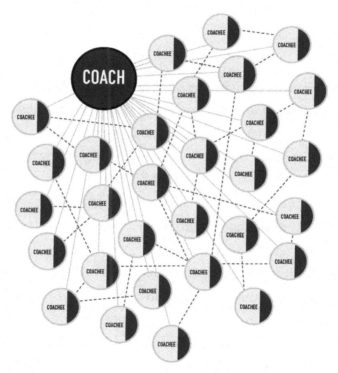

PEER GROUP COACHING
* Shading denotes that every coachee
also plays the role of coach.

As coaches, we know there's a pattern. Like we saw with Tina, nobody will change their marriage until they start working on themselves. Nobody will find a new job that is more fulfilling to them until they have the capacity to identify what they want to do next and why. We know the first place to start is always inside. *What do they want to work on first? Why? How can we leverage all of that Self-Awareness and move them into action?*

Tina, for example, finally saw via coaching that she, like Dorothy in *The Wizard of Oz*, had the power to change within herself all along! That she alone had the ability to step into the next phase, always choosing the next move. Coaching is about helping people break through their self-limiting beliefs. It can never be said enough: that's why we do what we do. Now, imagine that instead of impacting twenty people each year through 1:1 Coaching you could transform the lives of 200? That is the power of PEER Group Coaching.

TRIAD MAGIC

1:1 Coaching has two different aspects to it in the PEER Framework. The first is the coaching done peer-to-peer in Triads which makes up more than 80% of 1:1 Coaching in the PEER experience. The other 20% is coaching done between the group coach and the cohort member individuals. Triads are groups of three people, set up like a microcosm within the cohort experience itself. Members of a Triad often have their own confidentiality and rules of engagement, because if someone shares something with only their group of three, it stays within their own little group. As a result, people end up sharing powerful things in those Triads that the whole group may never know. And that's 100% okay.

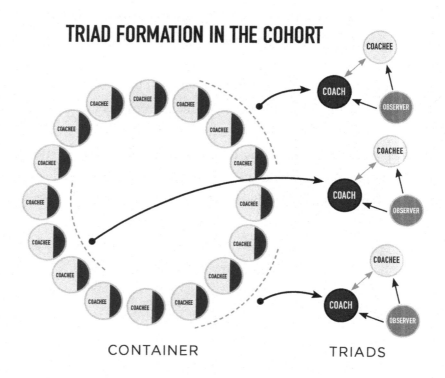

TRIAD FORMATION IN THE COHORT

CONTAINER   TRIADS

For Connie Eaton, one of the most valuable aspects was breaking into Triads. As a more introverted person, Connie did not necessarily feel as open to sharing right away in a larger group. She is not the type of person to become immediately vulnerable to all thirty people in the group, but in a smaller group she felt more comfortable.

Connie decided she was just going to put it all out there in the Triad and see what happened. She shared her dissatisfaction with her job and the questions for which she didn't seem to have the answers yet. Most importantly, she practiced vulnerability by naming her emotions, the overwhelm and frustration of not knowing where and how to begin. She decided to take this risk and be big and bold. That risk paid off.

As Connie started sharing, she heard herself telling her Triad the story of all the things she could not do. She had always admired her friends who worked *"Once we see our story, we cannot unsee it."* at big tech companies but had come to accept that working at a big tech company was not in her future. Later, she said that two things about that experience surprised her: she had unintentionally made herself believe she was not good enough for something, and the "fluffy sharing" really worked! It wasn't until Connie found the words to wrap around her emotions, to see, for the first time, the story she had written for herself about herself that she could see that it was simply that—a story. Once we see our story, we cannot unsee it. Using the PEER Coaching Map, Connie's Triad helped her dig deeper, past her Heart and into her Belly, challenging her to declare her authentic wants and needs. Not just what she wanted at age twenty-one, but what she wanted *right now*.

As Connie tapped into her own vulnerability, she realized it was in fact entirely possible that she could work at a tech company. She realized that, for some reason, she had been refusing to admit to herself what she wanted. She discovered that there is something in talking about feelings to other people that both protects and fuels the flame within.

PEER-centered group coaching really helped Connie critically think through and name her challenge. Just as importantly, she discovered what it was she wanted, and that it was she herself who had been holding her back from her dreams. It took Connie the entire nine months of EDGE to figure out she wasn't happy as a director, managing people at her company. She already had the skills and the network to work at a tech company. Now, thanks to her Triad, she also had the confidence. For the first time she had clarity about what her first steps would be and the accountability partners in her Triad to help her take them.

After this discovery, it only took Connie a short three months to secure a job as an Account Technology Strategist at Microsoft, the company she had once only dreamed of working for. With her voice and her vision in place, and the sense of worthiness that comes from transformational coaching, she confidently walked in the door of one of the biggest tech companies on the planet and secured her dream job. According to Connie, it was the Triad experience and the 1:1 Coaching skills she had learned in EDGE that gave her the confidence to take the steps needed to reach her dream.

As a result, Connie now feels successful, not only as a leader, but as a fulfilled, whole woman in a way she had never felt before in her life. Her mental health has improved dramatically, which impacted her relationships with her family in a powerful way. She still experiences the stresses and pressures of life, of course, but she learned about her purpose, and what it was that she valued, both in her life and in her career. She is living it, authentically and unabashedly.

We first introduce 1:1 Coaching in month two of the EDGE experience, because month one is really about building the Container. So as a best practice, we don't get into a lot of Relevant Content in that first month. Once the foundation of our Container is built, then we do a deep dive into content in month two. We call it the Immersion Session, because it is literally about immersing our cohort into the content that they will spend the next eight months focused on applying at work and home. Part of that content includes many PEER coaching elements. In fact, one-fourth of the time in the twelve-hour Immersion session is dedicated to teaching and practicing 1:1 Coaching. That is how important it is.

Because building an actionable network of peers is important to our Fortune 500 clients around Outcomes like retention, mobility and engagement, we also rotate our Triads at the halfway point of our longer group coaching experiences. This helps maximize the relationship-building and creates the space for people to practice coaching two more of their peers, who likely have very different personalities than their first Triad.

As the group coach, we first teach cohort members the tenets of coaching in the Immersion Session, then they practice the skill by coaching one another within the Triad monthly for the remaining eight months. When teaching people how to coach, I suggest doing a couple of small group breakouts to encourage cohort members to practice. In our EDGE experience, we use two tools we call the Coaching Map and the Observer Checklist.

There are three roles in a Triad: coach, coachee, and observer. In EDGE, we build in Triad time every month starting in month two. The expectation is that this group of three meets at a mutually convenient time each month for ninety minutes, separate from the peer group sessions, with the intent to coach one another. Every month they rotate through each role for thirty minutes so everyone gets to practice coaching and being coached.

THE TRIAD COACHING DYNAMICS

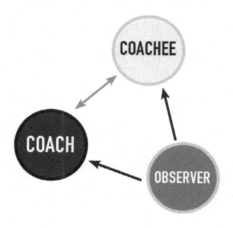

The observer role is critically important because for non-professional coaches, which is likely what your peer group will be made up of, this is a chance to see the power of coaching in action. The observer doesn't need to think about what question to ask next (as the coach does) or what their response may be (as the coachee does). Observers use the Observer Checklist we provide to give timely and relevant feedback to the coach. Each member of the Triad rotates in the roles, sharing their current personal or professional challenges, and experiencing what each role has to offer them.

Before we launch them into their Triads in month two, the best practice I would recommend is that you create space for them to get to authentically know one another. While they may have interacted in a small-group breakout at the Launch, there is a real chance that they may not have. In EDGE, that means we send them into breakouts with thoughtful questions. They rotate through and get to know one another—all the juicy, important stuff—by asking each other:

- What is important to you this year?
- What are your Individual Outcomes for the group coaching experience?
- Where do you want to go next in your career?
- What is important to you in your personal life right now? Why does this feel urgent?

As coaches, when we are coaching a client 1:1, there is always some type of intake where we get to know the client and the context. This is no different. Triad members get to know what's important to the other members. This practice helps them identify their needs, goals, and Outcomes. All these elements will be layered into their coaching experiences in the Practice Arena together. And like it did for Connie, this framing activity helps them begin to wrap words around their story, perhaps for the first time in their adult lives.

The important aspect is, of course, to simply create the space for your participants to bring a real personal or professional challenge and to help them practice the skill of coaching. I always remind them of the power of choice embedded into every group coaching cohort. That way each person not only gets to leave every Triad coaching session with practical next steps around a real challenge that is keeping them up at night, they also get to practice the skill of vulnerability. The fact that they share a real challenge is also most helpful for the person serving as a coach at the time because they get to work in someone's truth and contribute to their growth.

Coaching is an incredibly transferable skill. We create the space in the PEER group coaching platform to learn, and, just as importantly, practice this skill in the safe space. Then, we invite the cohort members to leverage their skill outside—to their teams, direct reports, matrixed peers, siblings, nonprofit boards, and more!

OFFICE HOURS

If Triad coaching is 80%, yet another powerful experiential learning tool (EXL) embedded into the PEER Framework is Office Hours, which is the other 20% of 1:1 coaching. This is the time when we, as the group coaches, are really engaging in 1:1 Coaching ourselves with a specific cohort member.

With our own PEER Group Coaching experiences at EDGE Leadership, we often offer Office Hours either as an add on after a 2-day group Jumpstart session or as a monthly standard that is included as part of the longer group coaching experiences. As you will see later when I talk about sales, we call Office Hours a "plug in" and allow our clients to purchase them in blocks of time post-Continuation, as well. Office Hours is not only a great revenue generator for external coaches (or credibility generator for internal coaches), but also a powerful part of the 1:1 Coaching element during the PEER experience itself.

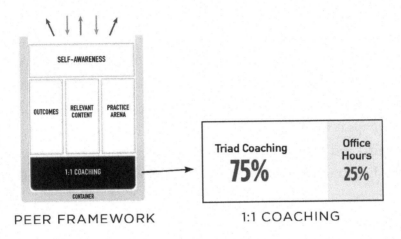

PEER FRAMEWORK   1:1 COACHING

When you are new to group coaching (but an experienced 1:1 coach), Office Hours can sometimes feel less like transformational coaching and more like transactional coaching. One of the first things you may notice is that you lack the time to build a deep relationship with each and every person in the cohort. For example, when I am hired to work 1:1 with someone over the course of six or nine months, there will be a session or two of intake and likely some type of assessment. Then we agree on a frequent meeting cadence and meet each time for anywhere between forty-five minutes and an hour and a half. (Personally, I like to block off an hour and a half because coaching has a very distinct end time, and in my experience as a coach for the last twenty years, you never quite know exactly when that end time will be.) Sometimes the client wants to go a little bit longer, but sometimes the client knows exactly what it is they want to do and are excited to do it. And if that's the case, I want to send them on their way and just give them white space to start acting on their next step. That is what traditional 1:1 Coaching looks like in my practice.

And as I said, group coaching has fewer touch points for the group coach with each individual, so it is easy to assume that the shifts in each person will be less transformational. And perhaps it would be, if the person wasn't *also* getting coached by their Triad and during the monthly peer group experiences. The PEER Framework provides a fishbowl effect. The fish (cohort member) is surrounded by water (coaching) every single day. They are literally immersed in it.

Office Hours looks a little different than the traditional 1:1 Coaching practice. Office Hours is the opportunity for the cohort member to be coached on their personal or professional challenges and learn about how to be a better coach *by being coached*. In Office Hours, often people bring a question about the leadership competency that may be a part of the Organizational Outcomes for EDGE or about how they can put together a strategy to apply the Relevant Content. Other times, we focus on one of the foundational elements of the PEER Framework, like vulnerability. We discuss what it looks and feels like to practice it in their personal or professional life. Most often, the Office Hours coaching is driven singularly by their individual

Outcomes—what they want most to get out of the experience. I follow the Coaching Map (just like Triads do for consistency) and dive right into how they are doing towards achieving that goal. *What is working? What isn't working so much? What haven't you tried yet but want to?*

I become more than a coach. I'm also an experiential learning partner during Office Hours as I work to show and teach them intermediate coaching techniques—*all while I coach them.* For example, a cohort member might hesitate in responding to a question I asked them. Instead of just sitting in the white space and allowing the person to marinate in it (which is what good coaches are taught to do in our typical 1:1 Coaching practice), I call it out as a learning opportunity: "Hey, did you notice how you did not have a ready answer right there? I invite you to look for this kind of white space when you are practicing coaching in your Triad." I might say, "Notice that your inclination may be to problem solve, or even ask another question simply because you are uncomfortable with the silence. In my definition, coaching is a 'working session' and progress is made sometimes *because* of the silence."

And often, like with Tina, I get a handful of people who sign up for Office Hours on a regular basis throughout an extended group coaching experience, like EDGE. In that case, just like with my typical 1:1 Coaching clients, I can move very quickly into transformational coaching, simply because we will have more coaching time together. But more often than not, I will average about two sessions with most people, spread out over the course of the entire nine months.

A word of caution here that I learned the hard way. It is easy to think someone did not get much out of the experience because they never had Office Hours with you, only to discover at Continuation, when they are sharing their Story of Impact to their executive team, that the PEER group coaching experience changed their life. And their coaching Triad knew all about it because *they* did the work, not me. That is as it should be.

I recommend that you structure Office Hours in thirty-minute increments. I'll do eight spots per month for a cohort of twenty-four to thirty. If a client wants more than eight spots per month, they can invest in another eight spots, or a four-hour block. I recommend you sell them in blocks, but every situation is different, so do whatever works best for your market.

Some of our clients even purchase Office Hours post-Continuation to support their leaders. High-potentials can experience a let down of sorts after a powerful peer group experience like this ends. Purchasing Office Hours offers a way for organizations to continue to support their talent. For external coaches, it can become a gateway to your private 1:1 Coaching practice. For internal coaches, extending Office Hours can be a way to increase your impact to key folks in operations. That's what Melanie Brittle, Learning and Development Professional and Coach at DPR Construction, did. Melanie participated in our Train-the-Trainer for the 9-month EDGE group coaching experience and created a platform to continue to expand her impact and support the growth and development of DPR's leaders with Office Hours.

Remember to always keep personal choice front and center. People can sign up for an Office Hours session if they want to.

Some cohort members will choose to engage with this element of PEER group coaching, and some will not. And that's okay. We encourage everybody to try it at least once, simply because they won't know the benefits if they don't. Depending on the industry, you may also find that people have many misconceptions of coaching, so be prepared to expand their mindset and share a tool and technique that will forever change their lives.

Office Hours can also look different for different audiences. At Duquesne Light Company, when Todd Faulk, Vice President of Human Resources, wanted to create an executive officer level PEER group coaching experience, we created the space for each executive to work 1:1 with their choice of executive coach, selected from a panel of well-respected ICF certified coaches, throughout the duration of the experience. Then the executive could choose how much time they each wanted to invest in their development. In fact, several members chose to extend the coaching engagement past the PEER group program.

"In Office Hours, cohort members learn how to coach by being coached!"

In the end, no matter if your version of Office Hours looks like our best practice or not, you simply want to create a safe space where cohort members can become vulnerable, understand how to coach each other as peers, and work with you 1:1, as desired, to explore their own goals and Outcomes at a deeper level. They learn how to coach by being coached! When cohort members learn how to coach, this PEER Group Coaching Framework becomes truly transformative, both individually and often on a company-wide scale.

Now that you understand how peer-centered group coaching works, it's time to sell the idea to executives and organizations. In the next section, I'll explain key actions for success when selling the PEER Group Coaching experience and alert you to a few pitfalls to avoid.

IGNITE: BEST PRACTICES

✓ 1:1 Coaching is the backbone for the whole PEER system. It's what makes group coaching just that: *coaching* and not training or facilitation.

✓ One way to curate this intentional developmental space is through monthly Triad sessions where the peers practice coaching one another around their current challenges.

✓ It is a necessary skill for coaches to hold the space for the room while simultaneously connecting to each individual. The flames of both are equal and necessary.

✓ Every time cohort members coach one another, they build relationships in the Practice Arena, reinforce the Container, embrace vulnerability, increase Self-Awareness, and practice applying Relevant Content. In other words, everything that has been built in the PEER Framework is touched by this coaching practice.

✓ 1:1 Coaching has two different aspects to it in the PEER Framework: coaching done peer-to-peer in Triads, which are groups of three people (the first 80% of the 1:1 Coaching element) and coaching between the group coach and the cohort (the other 20%).

- As the group coach, teach cohort members the tenets of coaching first, then have them practice the skill by coaching one another within the Triad. In the EDGE experience, we use two tools we call the Coaching Map and the Observer Checklist.

- There are three roles in a Triad: coach, coachee, and observer. This group of three will meet at a mutually convenient time each month for ninety minutes, separate from the PEER group sessions, to coach one another. Every month they rotate through each role for thirty minutes so everyone gets to practice coaching, being coached, and serving as the observer.

✓ Office Hours look a little different than traditional 1:1 Coaching. It is also an experiential learning opportunity for the cohort member to not only be coached on their personal or professional challenges, but also learn about how to be a better coach *by being coached*.

- Structure Office Hours in thirty-minute increments monthly in extended group coaching experiences like EDGE. I typically do eight spots per month for a cohort of twenty-four.

- Purchasing Office Hours offers a way for organizations to continue to support their talent and can be a gateway to increase your private 1:1 Coaching practice. For internal coaches, extending Office Hours can be a way to increase your impact to folks in operations.

THOUGHT SPARKS

1. *What takeaway do you have from this chapter? Why does this feel important to you?*

2. *How could you integrate Triad Coaching Practice Arenas in a powerful way to your current development programs? What could get in the way?*

3. *How could your 1:1 Coaching be enhanced by layering in experiential learning where your coachee learns how to coach by being coached?*

4. *Where could you see group coaching enhancing your work? How?*

5. *What is the first step to implementing it?*

6. *What could get in the way? Why?*

7. *By when do you want to take this step? Who could be an accountability partner to support you?*

SECTION THREE:
THE SALE

SELLING PEER COACHING

*"We make a living by what we get, but
we make a life by what we give."*

— WINSTON CHURCHILL

W hen I mentor coaches around business development to
layer group coaching into their practice, they often get
hung up on the idea of selling the PEER Group Coaching
Framework. Typically coaches are hesitant to step into sales in
general because, to be honest, most of us really struggle with
that part of the business. We may have preconceived notions
about what sales is and what's expected of us. Unfortunately,
just like the self-limiting beliefs we work so hard to shift with
our coachees, our own beliefs are often false and get in the way
of increasing our impact (and our bottom line).

In 1:1 Coaching, we coaches ask questions during the intake
process to find out if we are a good fit. Selling the PEER Group
Coaching Framework to or within an organization works the

same way. Just like people, organizations have strengths and weaknesses, fear and challenges we must uncover. The sales process is truly just like in coaching—we simply companion an organization on their learning journey; we do not push or pull to force something to happen.

> "The sales process is truly just like in coaching—we simply companion an organization on their learning journey; we do not push or pull to force something to happen."

I believe I can offer unique value at this juncture because before I was a coach, I was a professional salesperson. My first career was selling multi-million dollar surgical equipment for healthcare giants Johnson & Johnson and Bayer. While I was in college, I worked twenty hours a week as an outside sales person for a large staffing firm. I spent nearly a decade honing my skills in identifying prospects, framing business value, and closing sales. This chapter is not going to go into detail about how to do these things because there are tons of great sales resources out there for entrepreneurs to do just that. What I want to offer you is what I've learned as best practices for selling this PEER Framework to add to and amplify your coaching business streams.

When I was just getting started as an entrepreneur at age twenty-seven, I had a coaching company called Red Zebra Consulting. During this first foray into being a solopreneur in 2003, I was trying to sell an idea before the market was ready for it. As a Millennial, I instinctively knew that, as a generation, we wanted to learn differently inside our organizations. I had been part of large-scale training and mentoring programs at Fortune 50 companies and saw the limitations firsthand. I watched my peers tune out in PowerPoint-heavy presentations without true dialogue around application. I received binder after binder of materials with details that were not relevant to me. In both companies, my fellow Millennial trainees would get together after hours and discuss our successes and challenges applying the information—and our frustration with not being able to co-create it.

As coaches, we can have the sales skills (which I had) and the best product on earth, but if someone doesn't see the need—no one will buy it. The good news for you is I have been selling the PEER Group Coaching Framework since 2013 to Fortune 500 companies. And I promise you that now, especially in this post-pandemic world, more companies than ever see the need. My target market used to be companies with revenue over $4 billion because the value organizations saw in bringing together peers meant those peers needed to be remote—across a region, country or globe. Now, with companies embracing both remote and hybrid work models, even small to midsize companies are experiencing lack of engagement and connection with their employees. They are all in desperate need of a solution. At EDGE Leadership, our niche was DE&I, which has also become more and more relevant in the business space for smaller companies.

The other really important lesson I learned from my first solopreneur coaching business was to get out of my own damn way. When I had Red Zebra, I saw every other coach as my competition. I was not truly open to collaboration nor any best-practice sharing. I also had a self-limiting belief that I was too young to succeed at the level I wanted because every coach I competed against was easily twenty to thirty years my senior. Who would hire a twenty-seven-year-old coach? In my mind, whenever I didn't get business, it was because the company went with a coach who was older and more experienced. This false belief caused me to limit my sales success. As a result, I never broke six figures in any year of the three years I had that business.

But in 2013, when my husband Kevin and I launched EDGE Leadership, I did a number of things differently. First, I had grown in confidence and maturity. I gained amazing experience by spending seven years as an in-house coach and director of organizational development and was promoted to head of HR. Just as importantly, the market was now truly ready for what I had to offer. Now there were more Millennials in corporations—and we were loud. We were clamoring to co-create learning environments and be in consistent collaborative spaces with our peers. In other words, the sales pain points for organizations and group coaching had become more intense.

I also approached entrepreneurship very differently. Instead of seeing other coaches as competition, I went into business with the best of the best. I accepted an offer from Dr. Mary Shippy, CEO of Align Leadership, to incubate EDGE Leadership under Align's successful coaching and consulting umbrella. Not only did I receive an instant and accessible mentor, but I also was able to position my offerings to Fortune 500 companies because I now looked bigger than I actually was. I opened the East Coast office of Align and focused on trademarking the PEER Technology® Framework and growing the group coaching business with Mary's help.

Equally important to the business strategy was my personal development. Always more than my business partner, Mary Shippy was, and is to this day, a dear friend and the best coach I've ever met. Mary challenged me to let go of my self-limiting beliefs and leverage my youth as a differentiator, not a detractor. Thanks to her coaching, I began rewriting my story and saying to organizations, "You want to hire a coach that looks like the people being coached. That's me! Hire a young person to work with your young people." When I changed my beliefs about selling, it led to crazy success, expanding Align's total revenue fivefold in the first five years alone.

> "When I changed my beliefs about selling, it led to crazy success, expanding Align's total revenue fivefold in the first five years alone."

Most importantly, I learned to think differently about selling group coaching as a product offering. As someone who has sold this PEER Group Coaching Framework to organizations and audiences of all sizes and types, the greatest suggestion I can give you now is this: stop trying to pretend to be a salesperson—just be a coach. After all, it's what you already do well. Why not use your proven skills as the differentiator to shape your sales process? The truth is, the best thing you can do for sales is to lean into what you are already good at and coach people in organizations. The sales will follow—as long as you follow the process.

Every business culture and environment is different. One size does not fit all. Let the relationships you develop with the people and the success of the PEER Group Coaching Framework itself (which is thoughtfully designed to support your sales process), sell the experience for you. Once people experience PEER Group Coaching experience, they naturally become ambassadors for it. They will then find the words to sell it within their companies or to others as needed.

THE SALES STRATEGY

When it comes to selling PEER Group Coaching to organizations, there are two important things to understand. First, an organization has to be ready for it (and you have to know when they're ready). Second, you have to know how to best frame the sale.

Let me explain what I mean. Six years ago, when I connected with Todd Faulk, Vice President of Human Resources at Duquesne Light Company, he invited me to lunch because he had heard positive things about what I was doing with group coaching in the Pittsburgh region. He asked me to tell him about the PEER Group Coaching Framework. After I told him about it, I connected him to others who had experienced success with it. Although he said he loved what we had to offer, he told me his company just wasn't ready for it yet. I didn't try to persuade him otherwise.

Over the next five years, I stayed connected in Todd's network, not actively selling anything to him, just contributing geniune value as I was able. As coaches, we have to trust that the other person will tell us what they need (just like our coaching clients do). I stayed relevant to him but did not try to push (nor pull) in any way. Eventually, Todd gave me a call to let me know they were ready.

We launched a 9-month EDGE experience in August 2019 with a cohort of high-potential, mid-career leaders. It was so successful that the executive leadership decided to create a new officer-level group coaching cohort mid-pandemic in July 2020. After those leaders went through the cohort experience, they decided to invest in custom building a leadership model-based group coaching experience for their direc-tor-level leaders.

It is worth noting that the biggest selling points for the executive level expansion were the stories of transforma-tion told by the cohort members them-selves during the EDGE Continuation Session! It was there that the executives who were in the audience heard about the impact of connecting peers firsthand and saw an opportunity to grow and develop themselves. In addition, I never once posi-tioned any other type of group coaching to them during their pilot EDGE group. If I

> *"The biggest selling points for the executive level expansion were the stories of transformation told by the cohort members themselves during the EDGE Continuation Session!"*

had "pushed the sale" too soon, it would have been less effective. It would never have become an experience that would contribute to a powerful leadership culture change by an amazing executive team. I might have even lost the sale entirely. The company had to be ready for PEER Group Coaching, beginning at the top.

It's important to understand where a company is cultur-ally and if they are ready for an experience like PEER Group Coaching. The idea is to plant seeds, not push, because this is an experience that should not be forced (sound a little like 1:1 Coaching?). If the organization is not ready to move past their ideas of what L&D should look like, they will not be as receptive. It will not produce the same impact. It can also be quite harmful to empower mid-level leaders if senior leadership is not ready to support that empowerment. (I've seen it happen, and it is not pretty.) But when they are ready for a cultural change or a shift in development, the Framework becomes an easier sell, and the impact will be life changing.

HOW READY ARE THEY?

How can you tell if a company is ready? First, there needs to be some type of evaluation of where the company is, how open the leadership is to change, and where they want to see a shift in the culture. Finding out what change the organization does or does not want is vital. There could be a million different things the company is focused on. One company might want to expand cultural diversity, while another company might be focused on innovation.

Along with considering timing, I invite you to be careful with the language you use when framing the experience. Remember, just like in 1:1 Coaching, we meet people where they are, using their language. And, as we do when we coach leaders, you want to let the results of the Framework bring certain language shifts and the writing of new stories out in the organization. For example, I recommend that you don't talk about vulnerability and empathy before the organization defines the value of those terms—let that language come out of the PEER experience itself. That's what we saw at Duquesne Light, the company I mentioned above.

As you begin, identify what the company is focused on now and their buzzwords or internal language. An organization might be talking about talent pipelining or leadership development or executive presence (like Duquesne Light was), but after taking part in the executive group coaching experience, they now found themselves discussing the value of vulnerability and empathy to achieve those aims.

> *"When you are framing the sale, I encourage you to use language that matters to them."*

While we as coaches know full well that the best "professional development" begins with growing the person, some companies are simply not ready for "personal development" at work. When you are framing the sale, I encourage you to use language that matters *to them*. Use available data to get clear on the problems the business faces. You have to be able to understand the specific needs of the company, otherwise you will lack the necessary insights needed to generate lasting and transformative change within the organization and for the people.

The long and short of it is that there simply is nothing out there like this PEER Group Coaching experience. Even if there is a clear need for the results you bring, any time you sell something innovative, you have to find the right language to sell it. Trying to sell group coaching in the traditional training

"Trying to sell group coaching in the traditional training or coaching space is not easy. That is because you have to showcase how it isn't either of them. It's both."

or coaching space is not easy. That is because you have to showcase how it isn't either of them. It's both. If you try to sell snow to someone in the desert, they won't know what it is. It is the same way with selling the PEER Framework. It is unique and therefore requires fresh customized language that aligns with each company's needs. It's incredibly important to find a way to frame it so the client can best hear it.

That's where a partnership with internal coaches comes in. In my experience, the best sales machine for the PEER Framework is a partnership of two people—one internal to the organization or group, and one external. Typically, it is the job of the internal coach to frame the experience to the CHRO (or other decision makers) using the language that they know will galvanize action (for example, "retention," "mobility," and "engagement" are common terms that I've seen internal coaches often leverage), and the external coach supports the sale to ultimately deliver the experience. I first learned this quite by accident when I was paired up to design the PEER group development experiences with Michelle Buzckowski, whom you met earlier. External coaches support the sales conversation by asking questions and finding out the needs of the company, but it is the internal coach who is coaching the organization and understands the language and context of the company to help create the most successful frame. If you are primarily an external coach, focusing on your connections and leaning in to what communication internal coaches deliver will ensure your sales positioning is relevant and effective.

MAINTAINING CONNECTIONS

If you don't truly believe the experience will change lives, you will never be successful. On the other hand, as you've already learned, it is way easier to sell *after* people have experienced the power of it. They see the value, effectively communicate it in their words, and pass it along to key decision makers inside the company. I call that the advocate or ambassador sales model. In other words, you don't need to try to become a salesperson. I'm going to say that again. The very best way to sell the PEER Framework is that you are not the primary salesperson! Instead, create space for others to become PEER ambassadors and share their stories. When you maintain an authentic relationship (a skill we as coaches should have in spades), you will know that when they have the budget available and the company is ready— the sales naturally happen.

The key is maintaining connection. In all the years I have been in this business, I've only truly lost one client—and it was 100% my fault! It wasn't because I did not do a good job or because the cohorts weren't sharing success story after success story. It was simply because I didn't stay close enough to the client. We went from delivering successful cohorts inside one division of a large organization to piloting the Framework enterprise-wide. I was so concerned about supporting the cohort as their group coach that I didn't even think about the fact that my internal advocate and coach was also transitioning. We went from a budget being approved by Operations in that single division to an enterprise-wide HR department with more layers to it than even I was aware of as an external coach.

I failed to find a new internal coach when the VP of Operations (the program's advocate) moved on to another organization. Within four months, funding for the experience was reallocated. As a result, I learned that just delivering great metrics isn't enough—I had to make sustaining sales relationships and make keeping them healthy a top priority.

"Selling PEER Group Coaching is about building and keeping genuine connections, not closing deals."

Selling PEER Group Coaching is about building and keeping genuine connections, not closing deals. This work we do has a significant impact on people. As coaches, all we need to do is what we do best: create the Container for that impact to take place, and then let their voices shine. When you do it because you love to help people, great things happen! If you recall, the backstory for creating this PEER Framework began with me, as an HR leader, creating the space for sharing best practice with my working-mom peers in my spare time. I did not see what I was doing as a side hustle, and I certainly wasn't planning on creating a company with it. I just wanted to feel less alone.

When the national mentoring organization, Strong Women, Strong Girls (SWSG), approached me to build the pro bono group coaching experience for them in 2009, I was still employed full time as the head of HR at the industrial company I mentioned earlier. However, the volunteer work fueled my soul, and the work itself was valuable. As an added benefit, doing good in the world allowed me to beta-test the Framework that ultimately would become the foundation of my business and the book you are reading right now.

Selling PEER Group Coaching brought millions of dollars of business to EDGE Leadership. And as much as I wish I could say I was intentional and strategic about it, I truly just followed my passion for connecting people. Looking back, I can now see it was a powerful choice to do pro bono work with nonprofits who gave my work visibility. I engaged with leaders like Aradhna, who provided unfettered access to Guest Mentors, who in turn became powerful advocates and ambassadors for this work. (As a side note, those Guest Mentors were also usually at a senior level in a company that has a budget to spend.) It built my coaching brand and relationships with what would become my target audience. For example, as I sat on several nonprofit boards, often as the youngest leader in the room, and I would bring a fresh perspective to my fellow board members, becoming known as someone who had expertise with a Millennial audience.

After we launched EDGE Leadership, I put myself out there as someone who brings value to that particular niche. I delivered a TED Talk in 2013 called "#MillennialMuscle@Work." After spending seven years in the industrial space, I also wanted to bring attention to the importance of building a pipeline of women's leadership in male-dominated industries, so I started delivering engagements for that audience pro bono. As a result,

I met high-potential women from organizations and started building relationships with them.

You guessed it—those relationships often led organically to sales. In fact, the very first Fortune 100 company we landed as a client came from a fellow nonprofit board member who saw my passion at work around women and hired us to build a women's leadership group coaching experience for her company. Not only do we still work with them today, nine years later, but that single group coaching pilot led to the creation of two more group coaching initiatives—one with male leaders with the goal of creating more inclusive male leaders, and a co-ed group coaching experience for the graduates of the women's and men's groups together. It all began with the value I brought to a nonprofit board meeting about appealing to female donors and how we could do a better job of helping them find their voice.

"Now more than ever, with many team members working remotely, individuals are looking for ways to stay connected, facilitate knowledge transfer, and learn and grow together."

Who do you sell to? First ask yourself, who would be *your* target market for group coaching? Is it the same market you currently serve as a 1:1 Coach or L&D person? If it is different, why? What do you hope to gain by adding in this additional revenue stream?

The Framework truly works at all levels, so the field is really wide open. I have learned as a for-profit board director that many learning and development trends start with big companies, like Fortune 50 and 100 organizations, then move down to Fortune 500, Russell 3000, and eventually to private companies. Essentially, what works for big companies will work for the small companies, too.

The PEER Group Coaching Framework fits whatever challenge a company faces. It really is that flexible. Especially now more than ever, with many team members working remotely, individuals are looking for ways to stay connected, facilitate knowledge transfer, and learn and grow together. They want to feel like they belong. It can work for every company that is ready because the peer group—the people in the cohort—are the ones who understand the challenges. Simply plug any people facing any challenge into the PEER Framework, and it will work.

That said, we have to hold the process and relationship with an open palm because, like that sand at the beach, the tighter we try to hold on to a sale, the more it will slip through our fingers. We have to recognize where there is potential and discover specific needs, challenges, and successes—what's important to the company. When I first began selling the PEER Framework, I didn't start doing this intentional discovery process as a sales strategy. I simply wanted to help the people in the organizations. But, just like the intake process in 1:1 Coaching, it works as a sales strategy too—it's all about uncovering and amplifying their voices.

Here's a question I hear often: To whom do I sell the PEER Framework *within* an organization? It may surprise you to learn that I don't often sell to the CHRO or L&D. When I was the head of HR, I didn't have any time to take calls from new vendors. I was too busy just trying to keep up with everything.

Because of that experience, I learned my target prospect was *not* HR. It is instead business leaders in areas like Operations, IT, Finance, etc. because they are the clients of HR. They are the one the HR folks support. When organizational leaders need something (retention, engagement, mobility), HR leaders listen. They find the budget to fix their problems. As I observed and listened, I noticed that somehow the budget needed was always found when Operations said they wanted something! I quickly realized these other departments, not HR, were my strategic path to the decision makers.

"As a result, external coaches need to realize they are selling to the internal coach who is making the case for the budget to support the experience, not selling to the "entire organization" in general. It is a little distinction that makes a big difference. "

You have to remember, as an external coach selling to people within an organization, just like as a group coach—it's not about you. So keep your ego in check. It's all about coaching those internal folks to successfully sell the PEER Framework to decision makers in their organization. They can be anxious about putting together proposals and talking to VPs about it. More than anything, they need a coach to expand their capacity and hold them accountable to taking the next steps that will help them achieve their growth, which includes expanding their visibility and credibility by bringing value through group coaching to their organization! They don't need to sell *you*, necessarily. They need to sell the ideas for how this experience can improve their organization and how this success becomes a feather in the cap of their corporate career. As a result, external coaches need to realize they are selling to the internal coach who is making the case for the budget to support the experience, not selling to the "entire organization" in general. It is a little distinction that makes a big difference.

The internal coaches get you in, but once you have a PEER cohort complete, the entire cohort becomes your ambassadors. They are the ones who help sell sustainable group coaching vision to their company's executives. I know the traditional approach to sales is to "always be closing," but with this Framework, the cohort members close the deal for you once they experience the results and begin sharing the impact of it.

For the EDGE cohort, we encourage the group to spend the second half of the PEER coaching experience determining two things. First, what parts and pieces of this group coaching experience do they want to take outside of their cohort setting and apply inside the company as the "Pay It Forward"? Second, what will be their Stories of Impact? Then they have a one-hour presentation to the executive leadership team of their company at Continuation.

For the internal coaches reading this right now, this is a huge differentiator between the PEER Group Coaching Framework and "traditional high-potential leadership development programs." In old-school programming, we would have assigned the cohort a real business issue to tackle and would report their results to leadership upon graduation. While this sounds great on paper, we know it rarely plays out in a valuable way in practice. Instead, living our commitment to co-creation, we invite the cohort to choose any PEER Framework element, tool (like the Mastermind or Coaching Map), or Relevant Content area that they found truly valuable from the group coaching experience. They can then choose to work together, post graduation, apply it inside their team or department or even across the entire company. Group coaching is about taking information and applying it. After all, that is when information becomes knowledge—when the dots are connected.

> "Group coaching is about taking information and applying it. After all, that is when information becomes knowledge—when the dots are connected."

From an executive standpoint, this final presentation becomes not only a place for hearing powerful Stories of Impact but also an opportunity to see a return on their investment (ROI). Like we saw earlier with the executive team from the energy company, they get to hear from the cohort members themselves (not from HR in a PowerPoint slide) exactly what was learned, how it was applied, and what the results were.

Second, the Stories of Impact deliver a powerful element of the sales process at Continuation. The format we recommend is a TED Talk-style experience where cohort members share application stories of the knowledge learned from the experience. As I said earlier, while we recommend that you allow the cohort to co-create the guest list for Continuation, usually the direct managers of the cohort members, executive team, leadership, and the CEO get invited.

What the cohort members share at Continuation is arguably the most powerful part of the entire group coaching experience.

It is the culmination of the Container that opens the door for vulnerability and creates a space for sharing. Now executive leadership, managers of cohort members, sometimes partners and spouses, or even the entire organization can join in the Practice Arena, log on and witness the stories of transformation. Now the cohort members themselves, lights ablaze, fuel and inspire the flames of others.

Often the executive team will see the value right then and there, and your next cohort may be sold on the spot. These Continuation Stories of Impact and contribution to the company are so powerful that I have even seen executives text CHROs during the presentation to find out how they can continue the experience. (And those same CHROs then text their internal coaches!) In short, cohort members become the best advocates for the experience (and a key part of your PEER sales team) when set up to tell their Stories of Impact effectively.

A VIRTUAL REALITY

Sheetz had joined the Pittsburgh Technology Council, which is where I first met Grace Wirfel, Manager of Leadership Development and Talent Management at Sheetz, and had the privilege of introducing her to the PEER Group Coaching Framework when she joined our open enrollment EDGE cohort in January of 2019.

Sheetz wanted something to help develop an executive presence for women and enhance mobility and promotion rates. They audited several approaches. They really needed something with the capability to span both operational leaders and support department leaders. According to Grace, who had just spent nine months in EDGE, our PEER Group Coaching experience fit the bill.

For Kristin Smith, a Corporate Leader and Development Manager reporting to Grace at Sheetz, she and her team found the PEER Group Coaching Framework to be an effective methodology to connect talent development theory with techniques. Traditional programs typically teach participants theories and concepts, but not necessarily how to apply what is learned in the program. Kristin found the PEER Framework appealing because it had the benefit of immediate application.

Sheetz was built with innovation in mind, and the company culture values open-minded thinking and trying new and different things. Bringing in PEER Group Coaching was a good opportunity to demonstrate and practice that level of creativity and open-mindedness. Initially Kristin wanted to offer an in-person EDGE experience, but because their company spans across multiple states, they knew it would be a big challenge to get everyone together. Then the pandemic lockdown happened, which seemed at first glance to limit Kristin's plans in ways she never saw coming.

Kristin and I brainstormed options, including taking the experience 100% virtual. At the same time, she was already in the process of converting their in-person programs to a virtual platform. So Kristin and her team decided to give the full virtual PEER experience a shot. As I explained in Chapter Five, this virtual approach really allowed Kristin and her team to bring together people that ordinarily would not interact with one another due to geographic distance. More than anything, Kristin found they were able to effectively and powerfully build a network across the company.

Because the company was truly ready for the concept of group coaching, and they were willing to test a new approach, we had strong internal coaches in both Grace and Kristin. They wanted to co-create an experience that would focus on learning and application, so the PEER Framework was the perfect fit.

At this point, you might be feeling fired up and ready to sell the PEER Framework. However, you'll want to be aware of some common mistakes in the next chapter I've seen that are both easy to make and easy to avoid.

IGNITE: BEST PRACTICES

✓ Coaches sometimes struggle with sales, and may have pre-conceived notions about what sales is and what's expected of us. These beliefs are often false and get in the way of increasing revenue, so get out of your own way! Don't see other coaches as your competition, and be open to collaboration and best-practice sharing.

✓ Organizations have to be ready for PEER Group Coaching. It's important to understand where a company is culturally and if they are ready for an experience like PEER Group Coaching. The idea is to plant seeds, not push.

✓ The best sales machine for the PEER Framework is a partnership of two people—one internal to the organization or group and one external.

✓ Be careful with the language you use when framing the experience. Identify what the company is focused on and their buzzwords or internal language. When you are framing the sale beside the internal coach, use this language and available people data and analytics to target the problems the business faces.

✓ As an external coach selling to people within an organization, it's not about you. Keep your ego in check. Coach the internal folks to successfully sell the Framework to decision makers in the organization.

✓ The internal coaches get you in, but once you have a cohort complete, the entire cohort becomes your ambassadors. Don't try to become a salesperson. Instead, create space for others to become ambassadors and share their stories.

✓ Pay-it-Forward and Stories of Impact are two powerful elements of the sales process at Continuation. The cohort members themselves, lights ablaze, fuel and inspire the flames of others.

✓ Lean into what you are already good at, and coach people in organizations. Let the relationships you develop with the people, and the success of the PEER Group Coaching Framework itself, sell the experience for you.

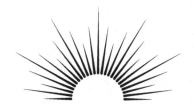

THOUGHT SPARKS

1. Who could be your target market for group coaching? Why?

2. What is the biggest challenge they are facing?

3. Is this the same market you currently serve? If it is different, how?

4. What do you hope to gain by deploying group coaching (impact, increased revenue, etc.)?

5. In the past, how have you viewed other coaches as your competition? How do you think this may have affected your overall success, both personally and professionally?

6. How can you identify whether a company or organization is ready for PEER Group Coaching? Have you experienced a situation where a client was not quite ready for coaching? What happened?

7. *As a coach, where have you struggled with sales in the past?*

8. *What are your strengths around selling innovations?*

9. *How could you find the words that would resonate most with your target audience around group coaching?*

13

MISTAKES TO AVOID

"You may encounter many defeats, but you must not be defeated. In fact, it may be necessary to encounter the defeats, so you can know who you are, what you can rise from, how you can still come out of it."

—MAYA ANGELOU

If you are an external coach who leads your own business, in truth you are also an entrepreneur. When you think about rolling out this PEER Group Coaching Framework into your business, it's important to consider the negative impact that mistakes can have on revenue.

On the other hand, if you are an internal coach or L&D professional, you are an intrapreneur, so to speak. You must constantly bring value to your CHRO and CEO and help the company solve problems. I hope I can bring unique value to *both* perspectives in this chapter because I have experience serving in both roles.

For me, the hardest part of selling the PEER Framework initially was that the internal mindset doesn't always shape the execution. There were times I handled sales well and times I didn't. Let's face it; you are going to make mistakes any time you start anything new. You are learning. You are going to fail sometimes. You will say the wrong thing, move too fast and lose business, move too slow and miss an opportunity—but the biggest mistake you could make throughout this process is not giving yourself the grace to be a learner. As time goes on, you will make fewer and fewer mistakes, but the mistakes you do make will have the potential for a greater ripple effect simply because your business is larger.

"The biggest mistake you could make throughout this process is not giving yourself the grace to be a learner."

The revenue potential for group coaching is exponentially greater than that of 1:1 Coaching. If you do this well, your revenue will easily eclipse what you've made in the past. In my experience, most external coaches have an annual revenue of low six-figures, usually under $150K with only a few of us ever breaking past $250,000. With the PEER Framework, coaches can easily surpass the million mark within a couple of years. After that, the sky's the limit.

You also need to be okay with the fact that you may never know why (and how) some of your mistakes happened. Not knowing is difficult. The mind might naturally start creating stories to solve the mystery. For example, you might start telling yourself you are not good enough, or that your lack of success is because you are being purposefully held back in some way. The trouble is, if you filter your thoughts through a negative perspective, you might only end up seeing your mistakes.

Give yourself grace to be a beginner. Let it go and move on. Get the support of a peer coach you work with to help you give yourself permission to let your mistakes go and be truly ALL-IN to make this PEER Framework work. That is the only way it will be effective and win for your business. Let's consider five important tips that, thanks to my own mistakes, you can leverage to avoid making the same errors.

TIP 1: CHECK YOUR CHECKLIST

One Tuesday evening, I was running late coming home, sitting in traffic with nothing going the way I expected. When I finally got home, my family was hungry, but nobody had started dinner. They expected me to do it. I was totally frazzled by the events of the day, and I felt like a failure. What did I do? I blew my top.

Luckily, my family helped me get some perspective. Kevin quickly enlightened me to the fact that I was the only one who had expectations about having a "good dinner" that evening. He was happy making a PB&J and watching TV. My son, Eli, said he could just make mac and cheese. *Neither* expected me to make them a home-cooked meal. It was I who expected it of myself. And in the end, it was I who ended up disappointed in myself.

You see, I had been operating under an invisible yet incredibly powerful checklist. To me, in that moment, what made a "good wife and mom" was having a healthy, wholesome dinner on the table.

Of course it had to include a meat, a starch, a vegetable, and ideally rolls and (on a good day) salad with homemade salad dressing. As I mentally reviewed that list, I realized it was absolutely ridiculous. I also realized something else—it was my mom's list. Those were the types of meals she always made sure we had nightly. I had been operating under expectations that were not my own.

After my "Tuesday Night Dinner Meltdown" (as it famously came to be called), I decided to change course and asked my family what a "good dinner" looks like to them. You know what they told me? All they wanted was that we all eat together, enjoying each other's company—and it didn't always have to be at the dining room table! We didn't even have to eat the same thing. At the next dinner, I enjoyed crackers, cheese, and a glass of wine. Kevin had two peanut butter and jelly sandwiches, and Eli had ramen noodles. Only after I identified the invisible checklist could I free myself from its expectations.

I share that story to help you as a coach identify your own checklist when rolling out the PEER Framework in your business. You probably have a few unrealistic expectations that will derail you if you're not aware of them. When I see people struggling with self-limiting beliefs, not feeling like a good enough leader, coach, sibling, daughter, son, or partner, I know they are likely wrestling with an invisible checklist. But the only checklist that matters is one specific to the situation, and every situation is unique. In my dinner preparation situation, I needed to base what makes a good wife and mom on *my family's* actual desires, not my own internal checklist that I had unwittingly adopted from my mom.

This checklist mistake is so easily made. For example, I knew I would be traveling a lot for work throughout 2018. Consequently, I wanted to intentionally negotiate my upcoming schedule with my family. I simply wasn't going to be available to attend all the school events, sporting events, scout meetings as I had in the past—everything had to be reprioritized that year. As the year progressed, I started beating myself up about not being present as much as I had hoped to be. So I decided to talk to Mary Shippy.

Mary listened to me complain about missing events like my son's baseball games, then asked me, "I'm curious, how important is that to Eli?" I got really defensive (which is how I always know when I have just heard something I really need to hear). "What would it look like if you asked Eli what he thinks about the situation?" So I sat down with my son and asked.

"I've been beating myself up that I missed your games," I told him. "And I wanted to ask how important it was for you that I'm there."

Do you know what Eli said? "Mom, baseball is the thing I do with Dad!"

At that moment, everything shifted. I began realizing that what I had written on my checklist of expectations about what it means to be a *good mom* was actually what I thought I "should" be doing, not what Eli actually ever expected at all. Asking *him* what makes a good mom and asking Kevin what makes a good wife dramatically cleaned up my internal checklist and saved me a lot of time, frustration, and heartache. Now I do this twice a year with my son (because things change often with children) and annually with Kevin. My relationships are stronger for it.

These unspoken, unwritten checklists bind people. It's what people think they should be, instead of what will help them evolve in the context they are in. In reality, sometimes the checklist someone is living under, like my what-makes-a-good-dinner story, was never theirs in the first place. So I invite you to "check your checklist" before proceeding with incorporating the PEER Framework in your coaching business. I invite you to ask yourself ten reflective questions as you do:

1. Why do I want to integrate group coaching into my practice?

2. What value do I hope it will bring?

3. Who is my target audience? Why does *now* feel like the right time to offer this to them?

4. What data can I find to support this need?

5. What industry/area in the company (external/internal coaches) could be a great place to pilot this? Why?

6. Who do I know in my network who could be a good internal coach and ambassador for me as I position it?

7. What does success look like for me in Year 1? (Hint: What is on my checklist?)

8. What is the first, small thing that will happen if I am headed towards success?

9. What is an internal mindset that could derail me? How could I manage through it if it does?

10. Who could be a good accountability partner for me as I sell (and ultimately) deliver group coaching?

TIP 2: LOOK BEFORE YOU LEAP

Imagine for a moment that companies are like crops growing in a field. A mistake I made in the past was to assume all crops have the same needs. But that is not the case. Some crops need more room for the roots to grow, while some can grow more tightly together. Some need more direct sun than others, and what is "sunshine" to one company is not sunshine to another. Some companies are flourishing in fertile soil while others languish in depleted dirt.

In short, as coaches we must recognize that, although we are always cultivating, we have to be okay with the fact that the PEER Framework is not going to be the right fit for all organizations at all times. *This group coaching experience is not the right fit for every company or every culture.* You do not want to sell this to a company that is not ready for it. One of the biggest mistakes I made was wasting time and money cultivating a company that had internal advocates who were excited about the concept of bringing personal development into the professional world, but overall the culture was not ready for the experience. You could spend months building relationships to sell the Framework to an organization, but if they don't have the budget, or if the culture isn't ready for it, it's best to find out early and let it go.

> "This group coaching experience is not the right fit for every company or every culture. You do not want to sell this to a company that is not ready for it."

The only way to know if the company is ready is to do your field work. There may be pockets of a company's culture that are ready, but the company itself might not be. Plus, no one knows an organization's challenges better than they do. I learned to trust that when they said they were not ready (like Todd at Duquesne Light), they knew what they were talking about. I simply let them know I would be there when the timing was right and stayed relevant to those internal advocates in the in-between.

There are a few effective ways to be present for companies when the time is right. Stay relevant to your internal coaches on social media. Check in with your connections periodically to make sure you know what is important to them throughout the year and make relational deposits into them. Remember the concept of the Career Growth Mountain. We have to know the strategic priorities of our internal advocates and what is keeping them up at night. Then we have to be intentional about bringing that value to them.

For example, I had an internal coach/advocate in a large Fortune 100 Company who I knew was looking to build her peer network in other organizations, as her long-term goal was to leave her company. So I made sure that I used her as a reference every chance I got with CHROs with whom I was pitching the framework. Not only did I benefit from having her share the successes we had created together in her company, but she also got the chance to meet new leaders and peers she normally wouldn't have access to. Win-win.

This only works *if* you know what is important to your internal coach advocates! And luckily for us, this is where we as coaches shine. We know exactly how to get to the heart of people's Outcomes and goals. Knowing those gives us the keys to the kingdom. The challenge is only in holding yourself accountable to follow through and do those bi-annual or quarterly check ins—just like I do with Eli. When he was eight years old, at the top of his "What Makes a Good Mom" checklist was my reading aloud to him. Now, at 18, it's more likely a trip to Starbucks while we sit in the lengthy drive through and catch up together. Priorities change. People change. Stay close.

> "Don't forget to converse with people at lower levels in the organization, because they will tell you the real scoop. They will help you find out if the upper and mid-level managers are treating your target audience well."

I invite you to also watch the CEO and leadership team. If the CEO is not modeling the right behaviors, chances are good they will not find sustainable funding for any kind of group coaching experience. Upper leadership needs to be able to demonstrate the change they want to see. Although they themselves may not actually be reaching the cohorts, they still reach the people who are. Look to see if the CEO and leadership team are walking the talk as it relates to what you want to cultivate inside the company with the PEER Framework.

The overall agenda is figuring out how to align what you do well with what a company needs. Because, just like Eli, what they need changes all the time. It is important to be in a consistent relationship to know how their needs may change or shift. Similar to what we do in our practice with 1:1 Coaching, it starts off with a spark of genuine connection, then discovering what success means to them.

Make sure to stay close with Operations (in my experience they always have access to the most sustainable funding) and keep up with relationships and contacts just to let them know you are thinking about them. It takes multiple relationships and connections to make effective, long-lasting sales. And don't forget to converse with people at lower levels in the organization, because they will tell you the real scoop. They will help you find out if the upper and mid-level managers are treating your target audience well. Over the last nine years, I have said no to three different companies who wanted me to create group coaching experiences for them. They had the available budget and upper leaders with hearts in the right place, but the mid-level leaders (read: the culture) simply weren't there yet.

As I mentioned earlier, I've learned from experience that the worst thing a coach can do is empower a small group of people then put them back into a culture where they get slammed down again. That is a sure recipe for disengagement and goes against everything we as coaches hold dear. When that happens, you haven't truly served the company nor the individual. And we always want to serve both. Sometimes that means you have to walk away from sales. I promise you won't regret it.

Here are five reflective questions to ask yourself as you build your Guiding Coalition of Ambassadors:

1. What is the value proposition you are bringing?
2. What organizations do you know who are ready for this? Why do you think they are ready?

3. Who do you already know in your target audience and if you don't know anyone, how could you get to know them?
4. Who do you genuinely like? (You will need authentic relationships to sustain success in any organization.)
5. What's important to them right now in their career? Where do they want to grow next?

TIP 3: MIND YOUR TIME

As you create a business development strategy, be smart about your time. Selling the PEER Framework generally takes more time than selling 1:1 Coaching. Just expect it. However long the contract is you are trying to sell, that is pretty much how long it will take to sell it. For example, if I am selling a 2-hour Coaching Circle, I should count on spending two full hours selling it. For a 6- to 9-month experience, I will allot that same length of time to build the relationship needed to sell that extended approach. From a time-management standpoint, when you are first starting out with the PEER Framework, be willing to spend up to half of your available time selling it. This will help you manage your own expectations and plan accordingly. (Check your checklist!)

"Plan your sales cycle with each company's budget cycle. Don't wait until they already have their budget planned out before approaching them."

For this reason, it is a good idea to start small and sell a concentrated experience first, like an Ignite Coaching Circle or the 2-Day Jumpstart. Your time is valuable, so you can get started by coaching your internal ambassadors to help you sell the smaller experiences. You can often find these folks in those who have already gone through your experience at an open-enrollment event or pro bono workshop or who have experience with your 1:1 Coaching. As ambassadors, they are an invaluable resource to promote the PEER Framework experience inside an organization and can save you a lot of time.

"You will have greater success ensuring money is allocated towards you when there are multiple ambassadors aligned and asking for it, so don't focus on just one person."

You'll also want to get the timing right for those internal ambassadors to make their ask. Plan your sales cycle with each company's budget cycle. Don't wait until they already have their budget planned out before approaching them. Essentially with group coaching, you are always selling for the following year. For my clients, money is usually allocated in October/November for the calendar year and March/April for the fiscal year.

That means I actually start selling the EDGE 9-month experience nine months before either March or October. You will have greater success ensuring money is allocated towards you when there are multiple ambassadors aligned and asking for it, so don't focus on just one person. For reasons mentioned earlier, I have found that my very best internal advocates are those internal coaches in Operations. I am focused on making relevant deposits into ambassadors the full nine months leading up to decision time *and* afterwards.

The great part about group coaching revenue is that once you are a vendor partner in a company and have a successful pilot experience, the funds will likely then come out of their operational budget and get allocated year after year. That said, even after a successful sale, you have to stay relevant to your ambassadors and what matters most to them year over year. Figure out what each company's budget cycle is so you are engaged with them when they actually have the money to spend, and be aligned in your messaging with those key folks throughout.

> *"What makes us great coaches actually makes us tremendous sales people. It is our key differentiator."*

As you progress in your sales, you will discover that in addition to creating space for you to exponentially increase your impact as a coach, the biggest value group coaching has is the potential for recurring revenue. Once your client base has been established, you are simply maintaining the relationships. Think of your initial time investment as an investment for the future and lean on your 1:1 Coaching skills with ambassadors and internal coaches. I truly believe what makes us great coaches actually makes us tremendous sales people. It is our key differentiator.

TIP 4: SCALING UP

One big mistake I made was when I began scaling up. Once a strong relationship with a company had been developed, I turned it over to another coach to maintain so I could focus on bringing in new business. This was a huge mistake. After I had developed the relationship, this lack of my personal connection really had a negative impact. It wasn't until I started losing business that I realized my blunder. You would never give a 1:1 Coaching client the tools you think they need to make it, then turn them loose. You have to check in on them and walk alongside them. The same thing exists for coaches and team members you add to your practice as you scale your growth.

You'll also want to make sure the people you add to the team know how to sell; otherwise, be okay with the fact that they will just show up as coaches, which means you definitely need to stay involved from a sales standpoint. It's important to know when to promote the experience and to whom. I can think of amazing 1:1 Coaches who are connected with a CEO, but that doesn't mean they are the best people to make a pitch to, so stage your sales accordingly.

It is also important to give yourself permission to do pro bono work to help you grow. Get on not-for-profit boards doing good work that aligns with your passion. Model the way for your cohort members by showing that you care about the world and the community around you. Bring inherent value when and wherever you can in a scalable way. In my first three years of business, I did one pro bono engagement with nonprofits and community organizations per month to gain exposure to potential advocates and internal coaches. I was selective in working with groups that 1) aligned with my passion at the time (empowering women and girls) and 2) gave me access to my target audience (Millennial women in male-dominated industries).

In most of my sessions, I made a genuine connection with one or two women who wanted to know more about what I did. Of course, I wanted to know more about them, their company, and their industry. I would schedule coffee dates and dig in. I would learn about their organization and culture (the "real deal" not what the company said on its website), and determine if they were a prospect. If they were, I would go out of my way to bring true value to the person to first, cultivate an ambassador relationship with them and, second, work with them as an internal coach to bring a 1-2 hour Coaching Circle in their organization.

"I look at each coffee date or phone conversation with a new soul as a way to live my personal purpose—to help people feel less alone."

Sometimes this strategy was successful, and sometimes it wasn't. I was okay with that because even if someone didn't become a valuable business connection, I was still forging a genuine relationship with someone I liked and hopefully bringing value to their life. That is at the core of who I am as a coach and person. To this day, I look at each coffee date or phone conversation with a new soul as a way to live my personal purpose—to help people feel less alone. Because I remained authentic to this, my network grew as my sense of fulfillment did also. It is only in looking back that I even realized this was a teachable strategy of business development. Like creating the PEER Framework, at the time I was simply doing what felt good, but it paid off in ways I could have never imagined.

After our revenues at EDGE Leadership hit seven figures, I simply did not have time to do monthly pro bono sessions.

It was time to reevaluate my checklist. Now I only do four pro bono engagements each year, one per quarter. I evaluate those opportunities through similar filters. I first consider my passion (which evolves as I do). If you would ask me today, I would say that I am currently most focused on being an ally to and advocate for the LGBTQ+ community (especially trans folks). Second, I consider seeing things through the lens of what is strategic to help grow my business. As I prepare to publish this book and help coaches like you bring this work to life, I am more interested in getting in front of coaches than I am in getting in front of Fortune 500 operations executives or high potentials, which was my focus for the last nine years.

In short, things change, so prepare to pivot your sales strategy as you grow.

TIP 5: HAVE A DEVELOPMENT BUDDY

One final tip as you scale is to have a business development buddy—think of it as your PEER accountability partner. Challenge one another to think bigger and better. This person can become a compatriot to talk to on a regular basis to bounce ideas off of, follow up on checkpoints, and talk about mistakes in a non-shaming way.

This person may be in the same field or even a direct competitor. I collaborate with plenty of folks who are competitors with me because I firmly believe in an abundance mentality. In fact, that's a big part of why I am writing this book. It's why I'm not holding back and instead sharing all of my best practices and lessons learned with you right now. There is always enough work to go around in this coaching space. I may not always be the right fit for an organization, but someone else might be. Rather than living in fear that someone might steal my prospects, I try to authentically embrace collaboration and authentically derive great value from those relationships.

Sometimes we can reset our mindsets on our own, sometimes not. In my experience, it is invaluable to have a peer to lift you up and keep you going. The person who has played this role in my personal life has also played it in our business—my husband Kevin. Before the concept of EDGE Leadership was even a twinkle in my eye, Kevin was the person who was my sounding board around new ideas. He challenged me to think bigger than I ever would, provided a perspective that was always (sometimes infuriatingly) different from mine, and most importantly, he held me when I failed and reminded me that he believed in me.

We can all feel the fear and do it anyway, but sometimes we can't do it on our own. Each of us needs a visionary who believes in us even when we don't believe in ourselves. After all, that is what group coaching is all about—creating the space for our clients to learn from and with one another. Why wouldn't we also do it for ourselves?

By leveraging these tips, you can avoid key mistakes that took me years to work around. I want you to succeed as a coach using this PEER Group Coaching Framework. *You can do this!* A lot of people are waiting for your help out there. Organizations need you to succeed and make this world a better place for us all. You're not alone, my friend, so don't be afraid to jump in and figure it out as you go.

You are going to make mistakes anytime you start anything new. It's okay to be a beginner. Give yourself grace to learn. Let it go and move on. Get the support of a coach you work with to help you give yourself permission to let your mistakes go and be truly all-in to make this PEER Framework work.

CONCLUSION

The world is not yet where it needs to be. That is reality. And this is exactly why those of us who are community builders, who work in this space of curating connection and belonging, have a responsibility to adapt our skill sets to what is most needed today. As leaders, we cannot lead organizations the way our parent's generation did. As coaches, we cannot coach now like we were coaching in 2000 or even the way it was done back in 2019. We simply cannot do it. The world will not allow it. Because for the first time in a long time, maybe ever, the world itself realizes that we are, in fact, a one single flame that burns brightly. We are not individuals—not by country, race, ethnicity, company, community, or role—we are, and always have been, a collective. We have a responsibility to continue to educate ourselves, to seek new opportunities like this PEER Framework, and build on them, always living in the spirit of continuous improvement. That, my friends, is how we change the world.

To ignite a flame, you need three things: fuel, oxygen, and a spark. Using what you have learned in these pages to help light the flames of others—to elevate the human experience and maximize potential—will also require three things: responsibility (as outlined above), courage, and hope.

You will need courage because you will be, without a doubt, challenging the status quo. Change always requires courage to go against the flow, to stand for a better future when it feels like most people around you would prefer to sit or drift. If you recognize that resistance is normal, you can prepare yourself to engage with courage as part of the process of bringing about radical innovation.

"Group coaching is exploding in popularity as more and more people awaken to the value of meaningful connection and all we can learn from one another."

Hope will keep you focused on what matters most as you encounter resistance. When I think about the positive change across companies and communities that has already resulted from this PEER Group Coaching Framework at EDGE Leadership alone, I know the potential for igniting the power of people is limitless. Every day, I put that hope front and center and let it fuel my mission to share it with the world. I encourage you to do the same.

Let the thought of group coaching cohorts multiplying exponentially and igniting the intrinsically collaborative nature of the human spirit motivate you to help unleash the fullness of human potential and make the world a better place for all people.

I recognize I come from a place of privilege. Even the fact that this book made it into your hands right now is part of my white, cis-gender, heterosexual privilege. There are powerful creators and inventors who do not look like me across the gender spectrum out there all over the world finding new and better ways to do this. I hope this book helps amplify their voices as we all learn from one another and ignite the sparks of possibility within each of us.

Group coaching is exploding in popularity as more and more people awaken to the value of meaningful connection and all we can learn from one another. Walls are coming down. Perspectives are changing. The opportunity makes it all the more important to exercise our responsibility as coaches to always be a learner first. To put

"In a room full of light, we no longer feel alone."

ourselves in places where we can have our own spark ignited so we can do the same for others. Together we can make the world a brighter place of belonging. Because in a room full of light, we no longer feel alone.

In fact, my hope is that you will use what you learn in this book—and make it even better. I can't wait to hear what you come up with. This is only the beginning.

Onward!

ABOUT THE AUTHOR

CHRISTY UFFELMAN, MHCS, BCC challenges the status quo. Everything she does, she believes in thinking differently.

Christy is founder and CEO of EDGE Leadership Solutions, an organization that curates belonging through group coaching. Christy spent the past two decades innovating in learning development with with a special focus on early and mid-career leaders, amplifying to include executive and board directors as she herself reached each level.

As a natural storyteller, Christy maximizes across genders and generations, shifts mindsets, honors individuals, and works hard. She is a recognized leader in creating connection and curating belonging. As a coach, speaker, and thought leader, Christy is on a mission to make people feel less alone by making connections that matter.

Named a Fierce Woman by Huffington Post, Christy learned her secrets and tricks-of-the-trade from experience facilitating tens of thousands of leaders in Fortune 500 companies with one hope—to curate belonging through group coaching and grow people from the inside out. She developed her PEER Technology® model to do just that.

Christy lives in Pittsburgh, Pennsylvania with her husband, Kevin, her son, Eli, and her two white German Shepherds named Theodore Roosevelt and Dwayne "The Rock" Johnson.

CONNECT WITH CHRISTY

If you're interested in learning more about PEER Group Coaching or working with Christy in the future, please reach out via Admin@EdgeLeadershipSoutions.com. You can also visit her website www.EdgeLeadershipSolutions.com or connect with her via social media!

- Instagram: @ChristyatEDGEleadership
- LinkedIn: ChristyUffelman
- Facebook: Christy.Uffelman
- Twitter: @ChristyUffelman

ACKNOWLEDGMENTS

In a sense, I've been watching tens of thousands of people write this book for more than a decade. So, I could not begin without honoring the cohort members who courageously shared their transformational group coaching experiences to be told within these pages. Each one bravely embraced their fears for this work to be brought to the world. I cannot thank them enough. I sincerely hope they find that this book honors the spirit of their contributions, journeys, and bright, bright lights.

For those cohort members who allowed me to share your stories, but whom I cannot name, please know you have my admiration and gratitude. I have learned so much from you, and I'm honored to be able to share your stories with others who will do the same.

To those important people who both personally and professionally supported me in this process—not only in writing the book and building the business that built the book, but in the evolution and growth of me, as a coach, a leader, a whole person, I thank you from the bottom of my heart.

Thank you to my husband, Kevin, for your unrelenting faith in my ability and freedom to be who I am and build what I build. Your partnership is my greatest treasure, not only at EDGE Leadership, but in our life together. I am equally grateful to walk beside you (at work and at home). I thank you most of all because you make me laugh.

Thank you to my son Eli who is the most courageous person I've ever met, for reminding me daily of the importance to live an authentic life and to stop working and eat every few hours. You are a good man, son, and I am proud to be your Mom.

In many ways, this work would not be possible without the rest of my family. Thank you to my brothers, Stephen and Karl, who taught me loyalty and trustworthiness, my mother, Elaine, and grandparents, Dorothy and Steve, Kathleen and Karl. I've learned about what it is to be truly seen for who you are—and loved—despite our imperfections. These lessons helped me realize my dream of building a group coaching framework that creates the space for others to see and to be seen, and to grow beyond their wildest dreams.

When I married Kevin, I inherited a wonderful family. Thank you to Marianne, Bob, David, Susan, Brian, and, of course, to their spouses and to all my nieces and nephews—it is impossible for me to think of my life without you—you are my family.

I was once asked how long it took me to write this book. One answer is twelve months. The real answer is that I have been concerned with the issues in this book for most of my life. For as long as I can remember, I wanted to help people feel less alone by making connections that matter. I've been doing it since on the playground at recess and in high school, where I was awarded the Girl Scout Gold Award bringing Girl Scout troops across Pennsylvania to share best practices and create space for knowledge transfer.

No one has ideas in a vacuum. I have been deeply influenced in my own thinking by a lifetime of work in and around coaching with many brilliant people, some of whom knew it and many of whom did not. I can't list them all, but many are referenced in the book, and I thank them.

I have been raised by a long line of powerful mentors, each of whom fed, watered, and shined their sunlight on me before gently passing me along to the next in line. I am forever indebted to Dr. Mary Shippy, CEO of Align Leadership, who incubated a fledgling group coaching model inside her successful global business, and who walked every step of this journey with me. Among many influences, the terminology of *PEER Technology* and *Practice Arena* were inspired directly by her. Mary, you saw the flame in me long before I saw it in myself. Without you, none of this would be possible.

Thank you to Michelle Buczkowski, Human Capital Strategist extraordinaire. Thank you for believing that it is possible to change the world. (And then doing it.)

To the incredibly talented coaches who have their fingerprints all over this work: Bear Brandgee, Felicia Byrd, Greg Mutch, Mary Beth Gallagher, Ashley Gibbs-Davis, Suzy Benson, Scott Wigley, Christina Barr, Dr. Peter Gabriel, Rita Williams, Patrick Murphy, Melanie Brittle, Emilie Gettliffe, and Christine Watkins-Davies. Thank you for being our test subjects in countless ways and for your feedback, ideas, insights, and encouragement. You will always be the first!

To the Remember the Amino peer group/inaugural Dare to Lead Cohort #1. Thank you for being my space to benchmark, practice vulnerability, and grow.

To the instructional design and support team at EDGE Leadership who built every facilitator's guide, slide deck, task list, checklist, and tool. Thanks to the Mother of it all, Marilyn Hoffman, and to Richelle Weiger, Beth Sheets, Kristin Riley, and Kathy Duziak.

And to Brad. Always to Brad.

I have had the extraordinary fortune of working with people who are both colleagues and good friends. I wish there was some way, beyond a simple thank you, to let the following people know how much they've touched my life: Kate, Liz, Abby, Amanda, Gina, Laura, Nicole, Christine, Jean, Maddie, Jenny, Angela, Andrea, Regina, Shannon, Rose, Dara, Steffanie, Kelly, Stacie, Jen, Amy, Jodi, Cyndi, Emilie, Kari, Amiena, Linda, Brienne, Kelliegh, Hallie, Megan, Marisa, and Cathie. You define friendship.

Thank you to my person, Andrea. P2P4ever.

Thank you to those amazing thought leaders and influencers whose work created a foundation for mine: Julio Olalla, Brené Brown, Marianne Williamson, Bill Burnett, Dave Evans, Kristen Neff, Tiffany Dufu, Byron Katie, Miguel Ruiz, Chanequa Walker-Barnes, Paulo Coelho, Carol Dweck, and Bruce Fielder. I honor your voices and hope I do justice to them in these pages.

Thank you to all who lent their name to mine by endorsing the book, and to all the advocates who continue to speak my name in rooms that I will never enter. Laura Ellsworth, Sylvia Fields, Carrie Coghill, Jeff Brown, Kim Fleming, Jeff Broadhurst, Leroy Ball, David Motley, Chuck Cohen, and John Surma. I wouldn't be where I am without your voices.

Thank you to EMPOWER: the very first cohort that began it all. Love to you, always.

Thank you to the CoT: The 2nd cohort who challenged me to think bigger and, just as importantly, taught me the limitations of peer learning. Thanks to Aradhana Oliphant-Dhanda for creating the concept of Guest Mentors.

Thank you to my high school teachers who reminded me of my value and my voice: Mr. Crossin, Mrs. Desman, and Mrs. Puppo. Because of you, I am here.

I owe a special thanks to those who helped me find my speaking voice. Without you, I may never have found my writing voice: Association of General Contractors–My first national speaking conference; TEDx–Lee Ann Munger and Jayne Houston; and Harvard–J.G. Boccella.

This book also benefited considerably from our many clients at EDGE Leadership whose names we cannot list but who we would not be here without. Thank you to those clients who gave permission to share their stories, both named and unnamed, and especially Todd Faulk, Michelle Buczkowski, Grace Wirfel and Kristin Smith.

Thank you to Meesha and Michelle from Red Tree and to Alyssa and Domanique from Moons and the ReBrand Lab for their brand, web design, and social media work.

Thank you to Sharnay Hearn-Davis and the Sisters Lifting as We Climb network. I am forever grateful for your companionship on my anti-racism journey. Without you, Sharnay, I would never have realized how important it is to live an anti-racist life and take such intentional action in my personal and professional circles. I know I still have a long way to go and am grateful for your friendship and mentorship.

Lastly, I want to thank the people who believed enough in this work to turn it into a book. Thank you to the entire team at StoryBuilders—my editor and publisher, Bill Blankschaen (for giving me a dream team of people to bring it to life), and to all of the great folks behind the scenes, who turned chicken scratch notes and a handful of cell phone pics into what you read in these pages. I thank you for your sensitive prodding when I needed to be clearer, for your calm and unwavering enthusiasm, rare levels of grace to enrich the content, and thoughtfulness to refine the structure. (And, of course, to Chris Winton for the introduction!)

When I first began working on this book, I knew I wanted to share the stories of our graduates and what I've learned from them to help other coaches bring more group coaching to the world. I didn't realize how much more I would learn and grow from the process of writing it.

My debt and gratitude are boundless. This train is only picking up speed from here.

Let's change the world.